PORTRAITS OF VILLAGE LIFE

PHOTOGRAPHS IN AND AROUND
BOTESDALE, REDGRAVE AND RICKINGHALL

Quatrefoil, 2019

RECORDING LOCAL HISTORY
Books in this series

Published by Quatrefoil
4 The Old School, Rickinghall, Suffolk, IP22 1HD
ISBN 978-0-9931706-4-5
© Quatrefoil, 2019

Printed by Gipping Press, Needham Market

Contents

Acknowledgements

Compiling this book has needed a great deal of work by every member of Quatrefoil. They are: Graham Clayton, Mike Doig, Sarah Doig, Sue Emerson, Sue Hardy, Di Maywhort and Jean Sheehan. Where additional skills have been required we have had no hesitation in calling on: Tony Emerson for drawing the maps, Charles Greenhough for enhancing and digitising many of the photographs and Peter Coles for scanning many of the photographs which we only had in hard copy. We would like to thank them for their hard work.

We would also like to thank the following for giving us copies of their family photographs and for all their help: Terry Andrews, Mr Aldous, Lilla Babraff, Michael Bailey, the late James Reeder Bailey, Mary Baxter, Chris and Marcia Bell, John Bennett, Michael Bishop, Bryan Boggis, Margaret Brown, the late Arthur Bryant, Gilbert Burroughes, Pauline Button, Brian Chandler, the late Kenneth Chilvers, Beryl Churchyard, Alison Compton, Michael Cook, Pam Cornell, Gillian Crossley-Holland, Daphne Culley, Ivan Debenham, Liz Draper, Dick Erith, Neil Flowerdew, D. Footer, Joan Francis, Brenda Green, Sally Green, Charles Greenhough, Brian Grover, Dawn Hall, the late Scipia Hawes, Tim Holt-Wilson, Justin Hubbard, Ken Liddle, Derek Lummis, Al Mathie, Beryl Martin, Patrick Miles, Tony Miller, the late Jim Moule, Donna Nevitt née Taylor, Revd Chris Norburn, David Orr, the late Dudley Orves, Cyril Piper, Ruth Powell, David Pratley, John Preston, Colin Ray, Kathleen Reeder, Kate Rose, Margaret Roubicek, Annette and Melvyn Saberton, Bernadette Sheehan, Mr Shemmings, June Shepherd, the late Audrey Simonds, Colin Smith, Paula Smith, Jo and Brian Statham, Margaret Stebbings and the late George Stebbings, Freda Strange, Hughie Taylor, the late Philip Unwin, Julian Van Beveran, Ivy Waters née Rush, C.J. Watts, Bob Wightman, the late Kenneth Wilby, Jeremy Woolcock, Jackie and Dennis Worby, the late Liz Yale.

Special thanks go to Mary and Ernie Baxter, Liz Draper, John and Barbara Foulger, Sally Green and Lesley Greenhough for all the extra help they have given.

We are often loaned photographs, deeds and other memorabilia which contribute to our local knowledge and to our collection of photographs. This is a good opportunity to thank all those who have helped us in this way. Unfortunately we did not have room to use some of these photographs in this book.

Special thanks go to: The Daily Express: 187b. The Diss Express: 137b, 139b, 149b, 191b, 230t, 238t, 240tb. The Bury Free Press: 7, 8, 139b, 149b, 175b, for permission to use their photographs. Ipswich Record Office for allowing us to use the Edmund Farrer photographs.

The numbers next to names below are page numbers. The letters next to the number; t=top photo, m=middle photo, b=bottom photo.
Terry Andrews: 15b, 70b, 75b, 76b.
Mr Aldous: 107t.
Lilla Babraff: 55t, 198tb, 199tb.
James Reeder Bailey: 180tb.
Michael Bailey: 53b.
Mary Baxter: 165b, 166tb, 212tb, 213tb.
Chris and Marcia Bell: 35b, 90t, 103t, 148, 154b, 160tm, 178, 188tb, 189tb, 224t, all from 225-227, 228b, 275b, 276tmb.
John Bennett: 14t, 26b, 56b, 128, 130tm, 131t, 132t, 161, 162, 195t, all from 216 -220.
Michael Bishop: 110b, 156t.
Bryan Boggis: 150, 151, 152, 182b.
Margaret Brown: 245b, 246b.
Arthur Bryant: 29tb, 41, 43b, 85t, 93b, 103b, 111t, 114t, 116b, 118mb, 127b, 134b, 154t, 184tb, 215tb, 263b.
Gilbert Burroughes: 44b, 93t, 159t, 185t.
Pauline Button: 153tmb.
Brian Chandler: 16t, 87tmb, 92b, 241tmb.

Cyril Piper: 260b.
Ruth Powell: 195b, 261tmb.
David Pratley: 101t.
John Preston: 158t.
Colin Ray: 33tb, 42t, 115t, 138t, 177t, 203tb, 204tb, 245t, 248, 249t.
Kathleen Reeder. 155b.
Kate Rose: 187t.
Margaret Roubicek: 141b.
Annette and Melvyn Saberton: 52t, 52m.
Bernadette Sheehan: 229tb.
Mr Shemmings: 163t, 244t.
June Shepherd: 236b.
Audrey Simonds: 9t, 19b, 27b, 50b, 56t, 57t, 68m, 69b, 73b, 208tb, 209tb, 224b, 277t, 278t.
Colin Smith: 39, 74tb, 75t.
Paula Smith: 181tmb, 182tm, 196tb, 223tb.
Jo and Brian Statham: 42b.
George and Margaret Stebbings: 206t, all from 266 to 275t.
Freda Strange: 210t.
Hughie Taylor: 254b.
Philip Unwin: 67m, 120.
Julian Van Beveran: 278b.
Ivy Waters née Rush: 168b, 205tmb.
C.J. Watts: 98tm, 211t.
Bob Wightman: 37tb.
Kenneth Wilby: 158b, 159b.
Jeremy Woolcock: 189tmb.
Jackie Worby: 108tm, 202t.
Liz Yale: 64t.

Introduction

Redgrave derives its name from the Saxon language meaning 'reed ditch'. The name of Rickinghall also derives from the Saxon and means 'the hollow of the people of Rica'. Botesdale means St. Botolph's valley but why this hamlet should be associated with the saint is unfortunately not known.

To the north, Redgrave is bounded by the rivers Little Ouse, flowing westwards, and the Waveney flowing eastwards. Between the sources of these two rivers is a small strip of land providing the only crossing place between Norfolk and Suffolk which does not go over water. Mesolithic people camped close to the river Waveney on the edge of the fen some time between four and ten thousand years ago. They left evidence of the flint tools which they made close to the present Fen Street. They were hunter-gatherers who did not settle in one place. Neolithic people followed and were the first farmers to settle in this area.

Fen Street, Redgrave, running along the edge of the fen was named in medieval documents and is probably the site of the earliest houses to appear in the village. Redgrave Street was known as Outhatch at this time and eventually became the main area of the village, along with Redgrave Green. This Green is now divided by the present B1113 and the land to the east of it is known as Half Moon Green and to the west as The Green.

Like Redgrave the villages of Botesdale, Rickinghall Inferior and Rickinghall Superior have been inhabited since the Mesolithic period with evidence of Neolithic occupation found by Basil Brown, the local archaeologist, in the field at the end of Fen Lane at the edge of Botesdale Fen. Roman pottery kilns have been found throughout the area which means these villages were very much an industrial area at that time, possibly transporting their wares to the surrounding region. The present lay-out of all the villages probably began in the Saxon period when the main occupation was agricultural.

Botesdale began as a hamlet of Redgrave. It had a common to the south called Micklewood Green which, in the medieval period, had houses scattered around it. Allwood Green to the south was originally a large common which was used by seven surrounding villages, among them Botesdale and the Rickinghalls, before it was enclosed in the early 19th century.

In the early 11th century the manors of Rickinghall Inferior and Redgrave with Botesdale were given to the Abbey of Bury St Edmunds by Ulfketel, Earl of East Anglia. Redgrave was an important manor at this time and throughout the medieval period. The abbots of the abbey had a hunting lodge in Redgrave Park from the early 13th century. After the dissolution of the monasteries these manors were acquired by Sir Nicholas Bacon. In the early 18th century they were sold to Chief Justice Sir John Holt and later that century they passed by inheritance to the Wilson family.

An important factor in the way Botesdale and the Rickinghalls developed was their location on the main route from Bury St Edmunds to Norwich and Great Yarmouth. Because of this, Botesdale market developed in the early 13th century, with its charter confirmed by Henry III in 1227. This was an important market surviving until the 19th century which meant the villages were trade and commercial centres throughout this time. In the 18th century the turnpike road between Bury St. Edmunds and Scole came through the two villages, carrying stagecoaches, post coaches and other traffic. The Street through the villages had become so busy by the mid-20th century that a bypass was built and opened in 1995.

Many books are enhanced by the inclusion of illustrations and this is particularly true of local history. Before the advent of photography the best sources for these illustrations were often paintings, lithographs and drawings.

This began to change when photography developed around the middle of the 19th century. It was an expensive hobby at first but towards the end of the century rolls of film replaced glass plates and in 1901 photography reached the mass market with the introduction of the Kodak Brownie camera.

We are very lucky in our villages of Botesdale, Redgrave and the Rickinghalls to have many old photographs taken by professionals and enthusiastic amateurs in the late 19th and early 20th centuries which show what the villages were like a century ago and help us to see how they have changed since then.

One of the earliest photographers in our village was the Revd Edmund Farrer who was curate at St Mary's church, Rickinghall Inferior in 1881 holding this post for six years until leaving to become rector of Hinderclay. For some time after retiring he lived in Rickinghall. It was then that he took a series of photographs, mostly of houses but also documenting some events in the village, such as the demolition of Robinsons' Maltings, which was where Jubilee House stands today. He dated many of these photographs with not only the year but also the day and month which is a great help for later local historians. The family of the Revd Blyth took many of our early photographs between 1903 and 1913. Other people have taken and collected photographs over the years such as the late Jim Moule, whose collection Quatrefoil acquired recently. Many people have lent us photographs from their collections for this book (see 'Acknowledgements'). These photographs are an important part of the more recent history of our villages.

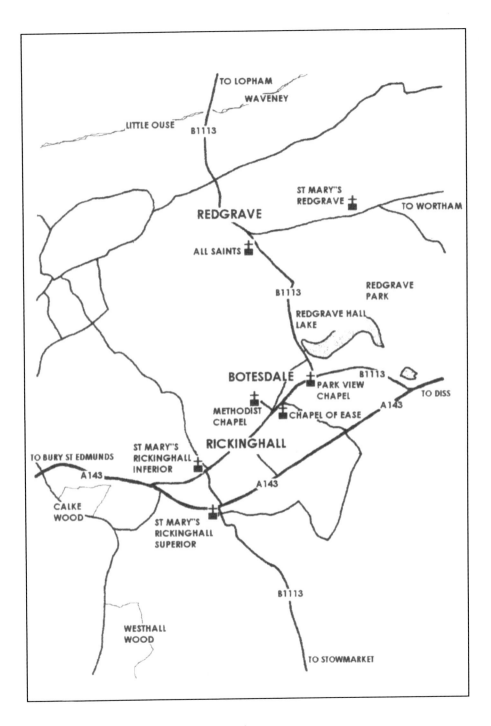

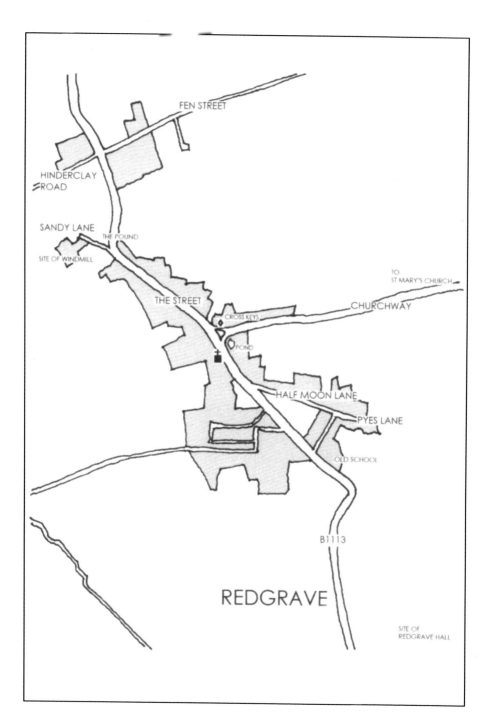

FEN STREET

HINDERCLAY
ROAD

SANDY LANE
THE POUND

SITE OF WINDMILL

TO
ST MARY'S CHURCH

THE STREET

CHURCHWAY

CROSS KEYS

POND

HALF MOON LANE

PYES LANE

OLD SCHOOL

B1113

REDGRAVE

SITE OF
REDGRAVE HALL

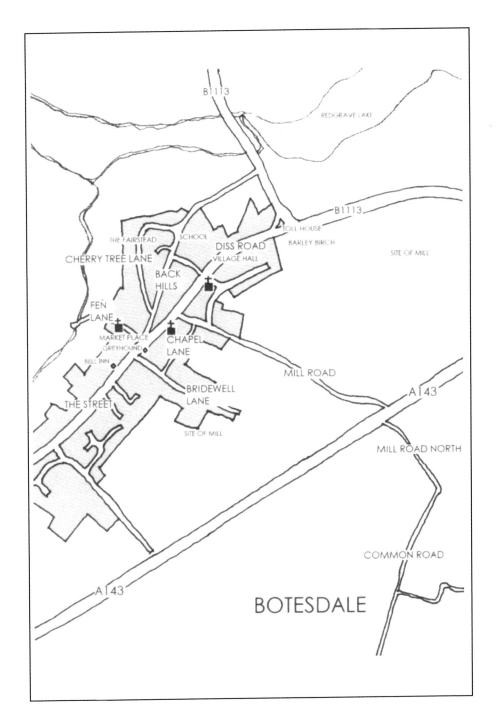

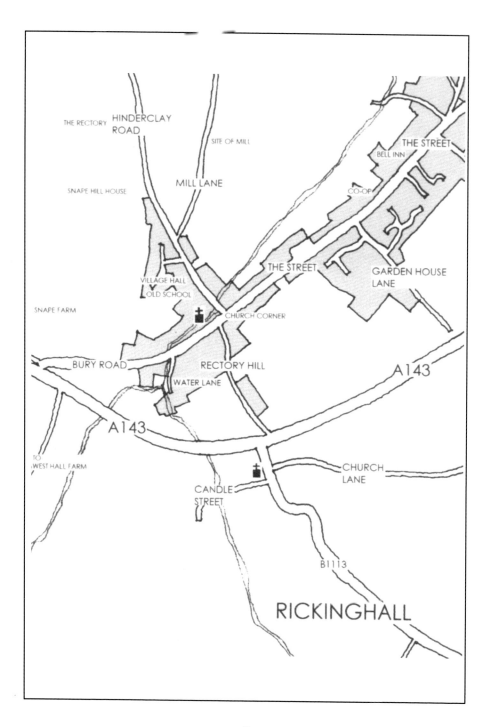

Chapter 1
Street Scenes

Redgrave

Visitors to Redgrave coming from the Botesdale direction, passing Half Moon Lane and following the road round to the right immediately see one of the village's most attractive areas. This is the Knoll, a small, mounded area like a miniature village green with a pond and in the distance between the trees in the upper photograph, the Cross Keys public house. On the left of the photograph is Redgrave Stores.

The lower photograph, taken in the 1970s, shows little has changed with the passage of time apart from the surfacing of the roads and the arrival of a bus shelter on the Knoll extreme left and a modern house on the right.

The view above is of Redgrave Street leading north from the Knoll as it was in the early 20th century.

A similar view, taken in the 1970s, shows some changes. The distant horse and cart have been replaced by motor vehicles, the road has been re-laid and Orves' garage and petrol pumps have appeared on the right.

Leaving The Knoll and heading northwards along Redgrave Street, there used to be an interesting building on the left. This was the workshop of Mr Pemberton, a builder, as it looked around the beginning of the 20th century. Beyond this is The Fox and Hound public house which became a shop.

Directly opposite Mr Pemberton's workshop in Redgrave Street is the Old Bakery. The house next to it is believed to have originally been the village's guildhall.

The photographer who took the photo below was facing in the direction of The Knoll, standing in a road leading to the mill which on an enclosure map of 1818 is marked 'Gallow Hill Road'. At this time the pound (for keeping stray animals) was situated at this junction. Redgrave Street continues on to the crossroads but is now called Gallows Hill. Beyond the crossroads the road leads to Lopham Ford, between the sources of the rivers Little Ouse and Waveney the boundary between Norfolk and Suffolk.

A later photograph shows how the road has been improved while the houses have hardly changed at all.

Returning to The Knoll and looking to the south provides a glimpse of the pond and on the right is Redgrave Stores.

In a similar photograph taken earlier it is possible to see in the distance The Mission Room which was built in 1897 and is now All Saints' Church. Almost directly opposite this building is an entrance to Half Moon Lane.

Half Moon Lane has a number of interesting properties bordering on Half Moon Green. The nearest house on the right is now called Oak Shades.

Slightly further to the south is the brick-built house which was once a shop.

Botesdale and Rickinghall

The main road running through Botesdale and Rickinghall is called, at various times, the Diss Road, The Street and Bury Road. It has various roads and lanes leading from it. Apart from those leading to new housing estates these roads and lanes have all been there since at least the early medieval period.

This photo shows how the village of Botesdale has changed over the past 50 years or so. The Street runs through Botesdale from the bottom right corner to the top of this aerial photograph from 1963. Towards the centre a road, Back Hills, branches to the left and the market surrounded the area around the junction. The building widely known as Chilvers faces onto the Marketplace with Osmond House immediately to the right.

The Drift heading from The Street to Back Hills can be seen with The Hollies on the corner. The field behind The Drift is now the site of the Medical Centre and St. Botolph's school. What is most noticeable in this photograph are how many of the fields now have houses on them.

A different view of Botesdale from 1959. Bridewell House in Bridewell Lane is in the foreground with a field around it. A semi-circle of prefabricated buildings, erected in the early 1950s, can be seen at the bottom of Chapel Lane, where Farnish House, built in the 1970s, stands today. A Roman kiln was found in this area by Basil Brown. The Street runs from left to right in the centre of the photo with Back Hills and Cherry Tree Lane forming a triangle with Rose Lane around the Fairstead to the north. Houses were built on the Fairstead in the 1980s. The Chapel of Ease and Chapel House can be seen in the centre of the photo.

An aerial photograph probably taken in the early 1960s shows Simonds' garage where Simonds Court and Oswald Mews stand today. Street Farm, with its farm buildings, is at the top right and the old Gospel Hall building, where Park View Chapel stands today, is on the left.

This photograph, taken from the top of Crown Hill towards the end of the village in about 1915, gives another view of The Gospel Hall on the right. 'The wages of sin is death but the gift of God is eternal life in Christ Jesus our Lord' can be seen on The Gospel Hall wall. The Queens Head inn is on the left.

Looking up Crown Hill, sometimes called Angel Hill, in the early 20th century. Crown Hill House is on the left and The Priory on the right. Botolph House is in the background.

Another view of Crown Hill from the Marketplace in the early 20th century. Aldrich & Bryant's grocers shop is on the right with Botesdale post office next door. Everyone has stopped to look at the photographer!

This photograph, taken about 1915, shows the Welsh Horse Yeomanry riding up Crown Hill. They were stationed at Redgrave Park at the time.

This photograph taken from the Marketplace looking up Bell Hill was clearly taken in the early 20th century, before 1920 when the War Memorial was built on the area between the roads in the foreground. An unusual feature is the gaslight on the right.

A similar early view from the Marketplace up Bell Hill. On the opposite side of The Street on the left it is possible to recognise the distinctive windows of The Greyhound inn. The narrow house next to it on the right was later demolished.

Another view taken in the early 1930s. The War Memorial was unveiled in 1921 in memory of the 61 men from Redgrave, Botesdale and the Rickinghalls who died in the Great War.

This unusual photograph of The Street was taken from the first floor of the Chilvers building in October 1979. There is at least one change from earlier 20th century photographs: the houses behind the phone box on the right which were built in 1973.

An early 20th century photograph looking towards the Marketplace. As will be noticed this was taken before 1920 as the War Memorial is not yet in place.

Two similar very early 20th century or perhaps late 19th century views of the Marketplace taken from near the top of Bell Hill. These photographs are both from family albums.

14

Another view looking towards the Marketplace in the early 20th century. The shop on the left sold hardware, later becoming the newsagents. The buildings to the left, as far as Fen Lane, are all in Rickinghall, however those on the right, due to the meandering boundary, are in Botesdale.

This 20th century photograph has the Marketplace in the background. On the left is a warehouse belonging to Robinsons Bros. which was later demolished. Hamblyn House is next to it.

The same view taken in the late 1950s or early 1960s. It shows the newsagents in the foreground with The Bell to the right with its inn sign clearly visible. Between the two buildings are three cottages which were later demolished.

This is a similar view taken in 1977 showing the bunting put up to celebrate the Queen's Silver Jubilee. The small building on the right had been a shop owned by Cyril Kemp. It was later used by the paper shop to sell papers in the early morning so people coming from the Botesdale direction didn't have to cross the busy road.

The Homestead possibly around the 1920s. The four cottages to the left were later burnt down by a fire which started after fireworks were let off nearby on bonfire night 1935.

This photo of The Street, taken in the early 1960s, shows The Golden Lion on the left with Jessamine House and The Anchorage in the foreground. On the right it is just possible to see the petrol pumps of Perry's garage. The Capstan cigarettes sign in the foreground was outside Elm Cottage, then a sweet and cigarette shop.

The view of The Street from Cloister Cottage looking in the opposite direction towards Garden House Lane. On the right is the row of three 19th century terraced houses making up Marsden Terrace.

This photograph was taken after 1929 because it shows the blinds of the Co-op on the right. The Co-op moved from the Marketplace to this purpose-built shop in that year. In the distance it is just possible to make out the distinctive roof of The Gables.

As a coach passed Jessamine House, Jim Moule took this photo from Prospect House in 1977. Perry's garage is in the foreground and Walsingham's garage is on the corner of Garden House Lane.

This shows the corner of Garden House Lane and The Street early in the 20th century with children standing in The Street looking at the photographer. The houses on the left were later demolished.

This early 20th century view is looking towards Garden House Lane. The road at this time had not been surfaced and had no pavement.

Here, probably in the 1930s, the photographer has taken a very similar position to that in the previous photo, looking towards Garden House Lane. Now the road has been re-laid and pavements provided. The Four Horseshoes alehouse can be seen on the left covered with foliage.

Looking west in 1976, The Railway Carriage on the left of Redholme was where Charles Birk had his shoe repair business. In 1984 the carriage was moved to Carlton Colville Transport Museum.

Looking from Chestnut View towards Garden House Lane 1979.

This photo was taken in 1976 looking the other way towards Church Corner crossroads. On the right is the cottage and workshop of Mr Bullock. On the left it is just possible to see the inn sign of The White Horse.

This scene, looking eastwards towards Garden House Lane, provides another view of Mr Bullock's workshop on the left with The Chequers pub beyond it. In the distance are the Maltings which were demolished in 1926 indicating that the photo was taken before then.

Looking towards Church Corner crossroads, this very early 20th or late 19th century photograph shows The White Horse pub on the left.

A later photograph of this scene also shows the bakery next door beyond the pub. It has two chimneys which means the photograph dates from before 1940 when the second chimney was knocked off by an RAF plane which went on to crash in the field across the road.

An aerial view of The Street showing, at the top of the photograph, Church Farm barn with a corrugated roof which was formerly thatched. The post office and Lamorna can be seen to the north of The Street with the foundations of Little Patches to their right. On the extreme left can be seen a granary on elevated columns to keep vermin from the corn. The thatched cottage in the centre on the south side of The Street was thought to be a former chapel. It was demolished soon after this photograph was taken.

A slightly later photograph showing Little Patches. The thatched former chapel had by now been demolished.

An early 20th century view looking eastwards with Robinsons' maltings and The White Horse pub on the left in the distance. Shepherds' shop and post office is on the right, in what is now Lavender Cottage. The post office was run from the early 20th century until the 1930s by Mrs Shepherd and after her by Miss Eliza Shepherd. The Shepherd family had had a carriers business in a yard behind the shop, now Harveys Close, from the 1890s and also had horse drawn cabs for hire. In the 1930s they had motorcars for hire and Edward Shepherd was a 'motor bus proprietor'. The business was sold to Simonds' Bus Company of Botesdale in 1935.

Same view at a slightly later period showing the post office on the right with advertisements for Castrol oil and a sign saying 'Cars for hire' relating to the motor business.

'Church Corner' in Rickinghall. Church Farm is on the left. The houses now called Breklaw and Rossendale are in the foreground with Forge Cottage just beyond. Mr Shemming's blacksmiths workshop can just be seen in the distance.

The same scene painted by Margaret Blyth the rector's daughter in the early 20th century. This clearly shows Mr Shemming's workshop beyond Forge Cottage and 'Shemmings'.

A view of Church Corner crossroads looking towards Bury Road.

Water Lane in 1968 living up to its name. Stanley Cottage is in the distance on the left and the Crooked House on the right.

Chapter 2
Houses

The villages of Botesdale, Redgrave, Rickinghall Superior and Inferior have a number of interesting houses from the last 500 years, the oldest dating from the late 15th century. In some cases these are easy to recognise, but many were extended and brick-faced in later centuries when timber-framed houses had become old fashioned and people wanted their houses to appear modern. Many of the buildings which were once shops, workshops or pubs are now private houses.

Redgrave
The Green

Rectory (photo prior to 1938). A rectory has been in this vicinity since at least 1433 when it was called Redgravegrene. The rear gable is the end of a medieval timber-framed house but listed as early 17th century (known as Rectory Cottage after division from the later part in 1980). Additions were made in the 18th and 19th centuries. The whole Rectory was put up for sale at auction by the Diocese in 1973 after the death of the Revd A. Hocking two or three years previously.

This is an early 19th century drawing of The Rectory before it was enlarged in the Victorian period.

Half Moon Lane

Black's (or Black) Cottages. Built on The Green, probably in the 18th century, as the town house (parish house) for four poor Redgrave families. The school was built in front of the cottages along the road in 1845. The cottages were demolished in the 1970s and bungalows are now on this site.

Bird's Cottage which was demolished in 1986. The Enclosure Map of 1817 shows the cottage was occupied by John Bird. Another Bird family lived here in the 20th century.

Bay Tree Cottage (formerly Debenham's Cottage).

Roof of Bay Tree Cottage being rethatched and the porch added when Mark Kenyon restored the house in 1987.

Juniper Cottage. The brick facing on this house hides a beautiful early timber-framed house called Guildhall Cottages in the title deeds of 1880. This probably is the Guildhall mentioned in the survey of the manor of Redgrave dated 1433 when the area was known as Outhatch.

Cottage on Orves' site. This cottage was probably demolished when Victor Orves built the large wooden shed on his land shown in the photo of his petrol pumps. (See page 65).

Railway Carriage. Colin Ray was born in this former railway carriage in Hinderclay Road in 1948, then known as Thorneycroft. It is now the site of the house called Lone Pine. Land had been bought by Albert Flatman to give each of his six children a plot. One of his five daughters was married to Arthur Button and they exchanged their plot with her brother Nigel further along the road closer to the river. Arthur bought more land and carried on his duck business there, now Gressingham Foods. Nigel Flatman, son of Albert, also lived in a railway carriage which had been enclosed in an outer skin of brick.

Botesdale and Rickinghall

The Toll House stands at the start of Botesdale village. It was built in about 1809 to collect tolls from those using the turnpike road which went between Bury and Scole. It was constructed using local 'Suffolk White' brick and is interesting because, unlike most Norfolk and Suffolk toll houses which are rectangular, this one is octagonal. Originally the road to Redgrave branched off in front of The Toll House but was moved to the present position in the 1970s.

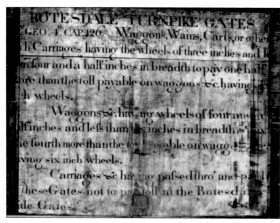

Part of the original Botesdale tariff board which was found in Botolph House, near Simonds Court, in 2012. This board would have been attached to the outside of The Toll House facing the road, showing the tolls which had to be paid by those using the road. Part of the board on either side has been cut off however BOTESDALE TURNPIKE GATES can be seen clearly at the top.

This pair of cottages was occupied by two roadmen. In the 1950s George Baxter lived in the right side and Ernie Pollard in the left. They were in charge of keeping the road through the village clear of potholes.

Basket Maker's Cottage painted by Miss D. Curle in 1921 before being demolished in the 1930s. It was situated on the corner of The Street and Chapel Lane where Park View Chapel stands today. This is where Albert Daines lived and had his basket making business until he moved to Cherry Tree Lane.

This photograph was taken from Crown Hill looking up towards The Priory with Street Farm beyond it. The Priory was called 'Tirpols' until the early 20th century when Dr Hannigan changed the name to The Priory. It was a doctor's surgery from the 1820s when Dr Robert Horner Harris bought it until the 1930s when Dr Hannigan retired. Between the two houses Mill Road leads to Botesdale Common.

A short distance along Mill Road stands Pond Hall photographed by Edmund Farrer around 1930. Later it was renovated and became known as Pond House. For a time it was the Rectory for Redgrave. Directly opposite the front of Pond House there used to be a large pond, often referred to as the horse or 'hoss' pond where horses from Street Farm were taken to drink and cool their hooves after work.

Further along Mill Road, not far from the present-day bypass, a post mill was built early in the 19th century in an area now known as Miller's Orchard. After the mill was pulled down in 1924 Mr Wightman bought the land and in the 1930s built a cottage using an old railway carriage. This building burnt down in 1941.

Botesdale Lodge is situated at the edge of Botesdale Common. It appears to have originally been built in the 15th or 16th century as a farm house possibly on the site of an earlier house. A large extension and coach house was added to the front of the house in about 1820 by the Cay family to 'gentrify' it.

The top photograph shows the front of the earlier building, the bottom left photograph shows the 19th century brick building on the right of the earlier building and the bottom right shows the 19th century building from the front.

Crown Hill House and Cottage stand at the top of Crown Hill. Both properties were formerly the Crown Inn from the 16th century until it closed in the late 19th century.

The first photograph shows Mrs Emma Kemp standing at the door of Crown Hill Cottage. In 1941 her sister-in-law Mrs Emily Kemp and her daughter opened a tearoom serving light meals at Crown Hill House. It was patronised by British soldiers and American servicemen stationed at Redgrave Park, as well as people from the village. Boxes of tinned food were often left on the doorstep for the cafe by the Americans.

The second photograph shows Nora Brier née Kemp standing in front of Crown Hill House. The doorway behind her was where the tearoom used to be.

Osmond House is a three-storey house built in the late 18th century. For many years Mrs Gowan had a tearoom, The Copper Kettle there. This photo shows it in 1977 with bunting for the Queen's Silver Jubilee.

A summer house at the far end of Osmond House's garden was constructed from clinker from the gas works which stood next door in Chapel Lane. Three houses have recently been built in the garden and the summer house has been renovated.

The Old Gas House, standing in Chapel Lane was the house of the manager of the gas company. It stood next to the gas works. This photo is of Arthur Bryant, his mother and grandmother taken in the 1930s.

At the end of Bridewell Lane at the point where the green lane starts stood an old cottage, probably built in the 18th century, called Hilltop. It had to be demolished and a modern home has been built on the site.

This photograph of Honister House was taken in 1977. Situated behind the Chilvers building, Honister House is a 16th or 17th century house. It was named by Mrs Mary Chilvers after Honister Pass in the Lake District where she met her husband.

On the corner of Back Hills and Cherry Tree Lane stood the police house, now the Corner House, built in 1855 complete with a lockup cell. It is not known who the police sergeant and his family were in this undated photograph.

The Old Saddlers, formerly called The Stone House, dating from the 15th century. Reference to a house standing on the site has been found dating to 1422.

Southgate Farmhouse with Robert Burroughes standing in the garden. Robert was a brother of Eric Burroughes who had the wheelwrights business in the building next door which had been a chapel.

Market Cottage was a shop until the 1930s. The Misses Curle sold haberdashery and sweets there but at the outbreak of war they left and the shop was empty for many years after this.

The second photograph shows the lovely 18th century shop windows being removed in the 1960s.

Astley House is a 16th century house that was once part of The Bell public house. It is said to have been named after Colonel Astley who ran a troupe of performing horses which he overwintered in the fields behind the house.

In the first photograph taken in the early 20th century, Astley House is on the right with The Bell next to it, covered in creeper.

In a later photograph Astley House is in the middle of the three on the right. Next to it The Bell is clearly visible with its inn sign just beyond.

Near where The Street reaches its highest point in the village is Hamblyn House which dates back to the 17th century. It was the home of James Hamblin Smith who in 1850 graduated from Cambridge University with a degree in mathematics and became a respected private tutor in Cambridge.

The photograph taken from across the fields by Edmund Farrer in the 1920s shows on the left of the house the warehouse belonging to the Robinson family who were flour merchants and maltsters and lived in Hamblyn House at this time.

The second photograph shows another early view of Hamblyn House and the warehouse next door and beyond a glimpse of the four houses making up Walnut Tree Place built in 1884.

The Homestead was called St George's House until the early 20th century. In 1935 Dr Ward bought the property. He had his house and surgery here. After the cottages next door burnt down he bought the land next to his house and built an extension for his surgery. Dr Ryder Richardson purchased it after the war and had his surgery here until the Health Centre was built in 1981.

Ridge House is an 18th century house which was later enlarged. The

coach house still stands behind the house. In the 1920s a Roman burial found in the garden was excavated by Basil Brown.

Marsden Terrace is a row of three 19th century terraced houses. The Reeve family lived in Marsden House in the 1920s. This photograph shows Emily Reeve in the pale blouse. It is thought the two little boys standing at the gate were two of her three sons Leonard, Reginald and Charles Victor.

This shows Prospect House being renovated at the time that the garage at the Pump House was closed and demolished in the 1980s. An old petrol pump is still visible in the foreground. Lion House across The Street can be seen on the left.

This photograph of The Garden House in Garden House Lane dates from the 1920s. It had been a public house from the 18th century until the early 20th century.

Returning to The Street, this photograph of Lamorna next to the Old Post Office was taken in the early 1930s.

Old Timbers and Flint Cottage taken in 1977.

Two photographs of Old Timbers from the 1930s. The first one shows Frederick Cook standing in front and the second shows Daisy Cook with her children Richard, Hector Cecil and Joy (later Orves).

Forge Cottage is a 15th century house owned in the 18th, 19th and early 20th centuries by blacksmiths whose workshop stood along The Street next door to the cottage now known as 'Shemmings'. The first photograph taken shortly after WWII shows Forge Cottage before the concrete block used for a gun emplacement was removed. A fire insurance plaque can be seen above the front door.

The fire insurance document dated 24th June 1793. In 1962 Mrs Thomas was given a certificate by Phoenix Insurance as the house had had 'continuous insurance' for 170 years.

A later photograph shows the front door had been filled in, however the insurance plaque is still in the same position.

Brook House is an 18th century house which was extended and re-fronted in the mid-19th century.

The Tuck family at the back of Brook House. The photograph was probably taken on a summer's afternoon in the late 1940s.

Three early photographs of The Cottage now called The Old Vicarage. These clearly show the diaper pattern on the roof. In 1944 pilots towing gliders, practising for the D Day landings, would look for this distinctive roof before dropping their towing ropes for collection from a nearby field.

The Cottage from across the road in what is now Low Meadow community land.

An early photograph of The Cottage taken in 1895.

This lovely little drawing of Hill House, now Snape Hill House, is from a sales document dated 1840 when the house was sold to the Norton family. The family were chemists producing 'Norton's Pills'.

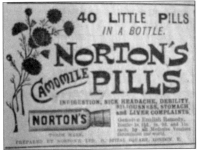

This advertisement appeared in the June 1896 edition of the Hartismere Deanery Magazine.

In the 1870s Charles Norton added a third storey and a turret. This was called the 'pill pot' by the villagers for obvious reasons. These had both been demolished by the 1930s.

Snape Farm was the farm of Snape Hill House. This photo shows young members of the Miles family in front of the house in the 1950s.

This early 20th century photograph of The Rectory is from a Blyth family album. The Revd Blyth and his family lived at The Rectory from 1903 until his death in 1913.

This photograph of Keepers Cottage in West Street from the early 1960s shows Christine Cotton with her baby sister, Carolyn, in the pram. It was formerly called Botwright's Farm. The well, which was still being used when the photograph was taken, can be seen to the left of the pram.

An early photograph of West Hall Farm taken in 1874 with Mr and Mrs Symonds, who farmed there at the time, in the garden.

Aerial view of West Street Cottage in West Street.

Next to West Street Cottage there used to be two thatched cottages which burnt down in August 1943. A spark from a fire started the blaze.

When the water mains were being replaced along West Street in the 1990s, evidence was found of occupation in the medieval period. A 15th or 16th century pottery kiln was also found. This site is not far from Foxledge Common where the Roman kilns were found by Basil Brown, which confirms that pottery was being made in this area over many centuries.

Chapter 3
Shops and Garages

In the past our villages were self-sufficient, almost anything people could not produce themselves they could buy in the village. A thriving market operated in Botesdale from 1227 with a fair held once a year on the eve and day of St. Botolph, 17th June, at which things were sold that could not be produced in the villages. Shops developed around the market place and along the village street in Rickinghall and Redgrave to cater for local people and passing trade.

Redgrave

Redgrave Stores (known as the Top Shop). This photograph was taken in 1890. There is a list of shopkeepers dating back to 1600 when Jacob Rix was the shopkeeper.

This photograph was taken just after the shop closed in 2005, prior to which an extension had been added for a post office.

The extension was converted into the community shop and opened on 23rd November 2007 by Bob Flowerdew, gardener and broadcaster.

This may be the smallest shop in England but it is very well stocked and staffed by volunteers.

Waveney Stores (known as the Bottom Shop).

This photograph was probably taken in the 1920s. Charles Fisher bought the shop in 1918 for £120 and paid £33.4s.5d. for the copyhold in 1919. He purchased the piece of land at the side for £25 after the field had been sold to the council to build the two houses between Waveney Stores and the Pink House. Charles Fisher had also bought Redgrave Stores in 1918 which he closed and ran his business from Waveney Stores as it was larger. Charles was the first person in Redgrave to own a car. It may be his car parked outside the stores in this photograph.

F. P. SHEEHAN

Grocery - Provisions
Waveney Boutique - Post Office

WAVENEY STORES, REDGRAVE
Telephone: BOTESDALE 259

Part of an advertising calendar issued by F. P. Sheehan in 1982.

In 1926 Charles Fisher gave at least one of his customers, Mr Orves, this order book in which he recorded purchases.

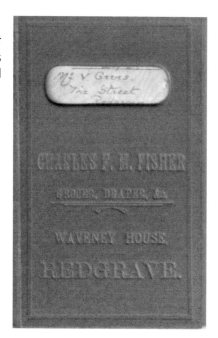

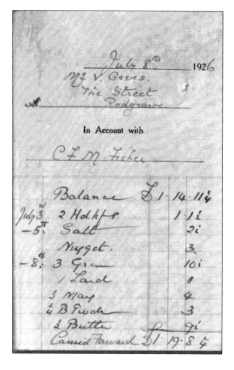

At this time many documents were only valid if they were signed over postage stamps.

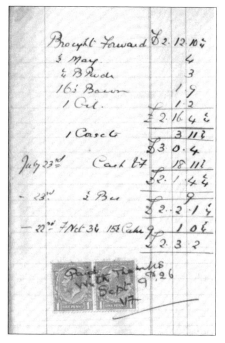

Waveney Stores in 1966 after being purchased by Jean and Frank Sheehan. Their daughter, Bernadette, is standing in the doorway.

Waveney Stores and Post Office when it closed in 1989, after nearly one hundred and fifty years of trading. The post office was moved back to Redgrave Stores.

Pink House. This house may have been the very first shop in Redgrave Street as the 14th century timber-frame includes two shop doorways.

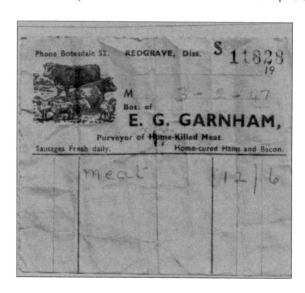

The Old Butchery was nearly opposite the Pink House. Ernest Garnham was the butcher from at least 1933.

Orves Garage. Victor Orves with Gomer's bakery delivery van in front of the petrol pumps probably taken in the 1940s. Victor Orves began to sell petrol by 1926 and retired in 1957. The business was carried on by his son Dudley until the garage closed in 1982. Victor had started his business from these premises by selling bicycles.

The windows of the garage shop can be seen in the background of the top photograph.

A petrol coupon issued to Mr Gomer which was not used as petrol rationing ended after the general election in 1950.

A bill from Victor Orves to Mr Button. This shows that in 1954 Victor was trading as a motor and cycle engineer.

The Old Bakery. The last baker to work from these premises was Archie Gomer. He had originally carried on his business from the building now known as Kent House across The Knoll.

Part of an advertising calendar issued by A.F. Gomer for 1939.

Jasmine Cottage. Scipia Hawes ran a small sweet shop here. She was born in the house in 1893 and died there aged 90. Her father, James Henry, was described as a licensed hawker in the 1891 census but by 1896 he was a hawker and shopkeeper in Kelly's directory and just a shopkeeper after 1916. Many people remember buying their sweets from Scipia after school.

Botesdale and Rickinghall

The houses now called Simonds Court are on the site of Simonds garage. In the early 19th century this site had been where Revd Joseph Haddock established a school. It was a grocers shop in the late 19th century until 1886 run by the Thompson family. In the late 19th and early years of the 20th century Walter Hart, a carriage builder, had his business here. Sometime later E. J. Aves had a motor repair shop which was taken over by Mr Ossie Simonds in the 1930s.

Mr Ossie Simonds is standing in the centre with Mrs Rosalind Simonds to his right.

Simonds' window

Bank House in Botesdale was home to various banks in the 19th and 20th centuries. In the 1850s it was Harveys and Hudsons Bank but by the 1890s it had become Gurneys Bank followed by Barclays in 1896. Charles Taylor was the bank manager and was still working in 1901 however by the 1911 census he had retired.

Barclays Bank rented Number 1 Pound Farm in Rickinghall from 1976 until 1991. It only opened one or two days a week.

Sage's Fish & Chip shop. The business has been in the same family for over 50 years. Until the early 1990s the fish and chips were still being cooked on a coal fired range.

This photograph shows, on the right, the building occupied by boot and shoemaker Mr Sparrow next to The Greyhound inn. Mr Gilbert Ashford later took over the business. The shop closed in about 1943 and was later demolished.

Bridewell House on the corner of Bridewell Lane and the Marketplace. Miss Green had a grocers shop. The building was sold after her death in the 1940s for £200.

The man standing outside the shop was called 'Chummy' but it is not known if this was a nickname or if he had anything to do with the shop. It is said he was a money lender.

The Chilvers building was built in the late 18th century by the Munns family who were grocers. In the early 20th century it was a garage, and John Harvey had a brush making business here from the late 19th to the early 20th century. In 1935 Mr & Mrs Chilvers bought the building and moved their haberdashery shop from Kent House in Rickinghall. The Chilvers family had this shop until the 1980s when Kenneth and Mary Chilvers retired. Since then it has been home to many different shops.

This photograph shows Mr Last's butchers shop in 1977. Like many butchers shops at this time it had an abattoir behind the shop. In the early 1990s when Mr & Mrs Cook were the butchers here changes in legislation eventually made it too costly to carry on and the shop and abattoir finally closed.

The Newsagent. There has been a shop on this site for many years. At one time it was a hardware shop then a newsagents. Mr & Mrs Kerry ran it for many years in the 20th century. In 2014 the post office moved from across the road into the newsagents but in 2016 the owner had to close both businesses due to ill health. Note the building on the right was later demolished some time after this photograph was taken.

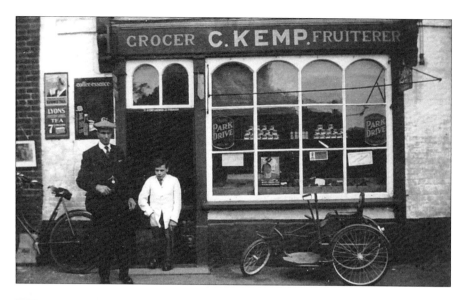

Cyril Kemp had his grocers shop in Hamblyn House which he had taken over from Mr Forder. This photo was taken in 1939. The second photo shows Norah Brier née Kemp outside the shop.

Cyril later moved his business across the road to the small building shown above.

By the time of this photograph the small building was being used by the newsagents across the road to sell newspapers.

This shop, now Faiths, was a butchers shop for many years. In 1839 Richard Wiseman, a butcher, was occupying the building. In 1866 another butcher, William Warren bought it. His son Stephen carried on the business. Stephen's eldest son, William, was killed in WWI and his other son, Noel, took over the business. Noel retired in the 1960s.

The top photograph, from early in the 20th century, shows meat hanging outside the shop. The lower photograph shows Noel standing in front of the shop.

The first local Co-op was in the Chilvers building in the Marketplace. In 1929 it moved to a purpose-built shop on The Street directly in front of the present Co-op. To the right of the shop there were two cottages owned by the Co-op one of which was for the manager. All these were demolished to make way for the present building which opened in February 2003.

In this photograph the Co-op can be seen trading in the Chilvers building just before the business relocated in 1929.

This photograph shows the Co-op just after it was built in Rickinghall.

This photograph shows, on the left, workmen preparing access to the new Co-op.

This shows the Co-op just before it was demolished. The two houses, one of which was the manager's house, can be seen beyond the shop.

There had been a grocers shop in Jessamine House since at least the early 19th century when Thomas Jolly, a grocer, was the occupier. It appears that William Street who bought the property in 1845 also had a grocers shop and possibly a pharmacy there. In the early 20th century Aldrich & Bryant had a shop in Botesdale Marketplace and another in Jessamine House in Rickinghall. The Rickinghall shop then moved across the road to purpose-built premises now called Pavilion House.

The photograph shows the Aldrich & Bryant shop in Jessamine House.

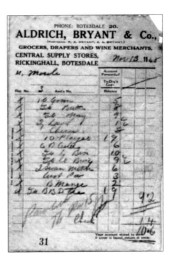

A bill from 1915.   A bill from 1948.

This photograph shows staff of the Aldrich & Bryant shop outside the new premises.

In the second photograph the people are from left to right: Charles Adcock, unknown, Murial Frost, Poppy Salt, David Martin, Mr Pearce, Miss Pearce who became Mrs Bunning.

After Aldrich & Bryant moved, the shop in Jessamine House became The Rickinghall Supply Stores. This photograph shows it in the 1930s with the shop assistants. Miss Kate Pigg is the girl standing in the middle. She later became Mrs Davey and ran the shop on the corner of Rectory Hill and The Street.

After Aldrich & Bryant sold the shop, Mr Warner took it over as a general store. A photograph of Warners shop in the 1980s. It is now called Pavilion House.

An aerial view of Perrys garage in the late 1950s with the garage buildings in the background. The garage had been built in front of the house, later called The Pump House, in 1926 and demolished in the 1980s. A small grocers shop can be seen at the end of Prospect House. The housing development, Ryders Way, was built in the 1980s behind the Pump House after the garage buildings had been demolished. Ryders Way was named after Dr Ryder Richardson.

A series of four photos taken in 1926 and 1927 by Revd Edmund Farrer showing the house being repaired and the garage built in front of it.

Taken on 11th June 1926

Taken on 12th June 1926

Taken on 15th June 1926

Taken on 18th April 1927

A later photograph of the garage just before being demolished in the 1980s. Warners shop is in the background.

Frank Alford, a baker and confectioner, had his business in Bothwell House in the early 19th century, later moving to the building where the Blue Orchid is today, on the corner across from the Chapel House.

Elm Cottage was built between 1475 and 1500 and was often used as a shop. The first shopkeeper was William Wiffen, a baker, who lived there for about 30 years until his death in 1661. He was followed by Henry Stanton, a grocer in 1662, the first of several members of the Stanton family who continued the business until about 1700. Sometime probably around the 1940s Harry and Emma Banham set up a shop selling sweets and cigarettes before Elm Cottage became a private residence in 1968. The photograph shows Audrey and June Banham who were foster daughters of the Banhams outside the shop.

The stray animal pound was situated on the corner of The Street and Garden House Lane. In the 1920s George Tacon Chapman built a garage and cycle repair shop on the site. Billy Walsingham bought the garage in the 1930s. It remained a garage until the then owner Mr Johnson sold it for redevelopment in 1988 when Walsingham Mews was built.

The first photograph shows the garage when run by Mr Chapman with Ossie Simonds the man in the centre.

The second photograph shows Mr Walsingham's cars for sale.

This shows the garage in 1964.

The two lower photographs on this page show the site after the garage had been demolished and the start of Walsingham Mews being built.

In the mid-20th century a railway carriage was situated in the garden next to Redholme. It was owned by Charles Birk who made and repaired boots and shoes there. The carriage was removed in 1984 and is now in Carlton Colville Transport Museum near Lowestoft.

Shaw's Fish & Chips and Bygones antique shop were situated in the garden of Whitegate. The wooden building was the Fish & Chip shop. They were cooked on a coal fire and were, apparently, very good. The small brick building had been a sweet shop in the 1930s but after the war it became Bygones.

The extension on the cottage now called Daisy Cottage was a butchers for many years. It was first owned by Mr Howard then Mr Ostler. After this it was Mastertons electrical shop, followed by Ted Smith's electrical shop. It is now a hairdressers, Cut Above.

The first photograph shows Mr Howard's butchers shop in the 1920s or 30s the second shows Mr Smith's electrical shop in 1977.

In 1926 Rosetta Fellingham opened a sweet and tobacco shop which she ran for over 40 years, finally closing it in 1971. It is now a private residence called Glenfield, part of a terrace of three houses.

Chard's Store. It appears that this building has been a shop from early in the 19th century. In 1830 John Foulger, a chemist, was here. In the early 20th century Miss Self ran it as a general grocery store. It appears that the post office moved across from Lavender Cottage in the late 1930s. Mr Stone had the shop and post office at the time. Mr & Mrs Harry Chard took both over from him. These were closed when they retired in 1985.

Chapter 4
Working Life

As well as garages and shops there were many other occupations and businesses in our villages. By the mid-17th century windmills were becoming widespread and several were built locally, usually on higher ground on the outskirts of the villages. In the villages larger maltings and warehouses also appeared. This, and the increasing need to move goods, led to an expansion of related trades such as builders, wheelwrights and blacksmiths.

Redgrave Mill. The mill was built about 1816. Henry Wright purchased the mill in 1866 and when he died in 1903 it was bought by Sidney Witton. This photograph may have been taken around this time as there is something fixed to the wall which may be a 'For Sale' poster.

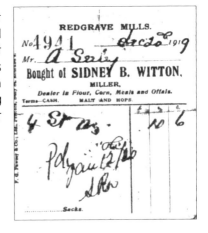

Bill from Sidney Witton dated 1919.

John Pettit bought the mill in 1923. The following year, only two days after John returned from his honeymoon, the mill burnt down. The fire was discovered in the engine house and spread rapidly to the tower mill, which was painted with tar, gutting it within an hour. The fire engine from Diss was called but no horses could be found to pull it. The fire was discovered at 4pm, and the Hopton fire brigade arrived at 7.30pm with their manual pump, but it was discovered the hosepipe was full of holes. Meanwhile villagers had formed a human chain to pass buckets of water from the pond at Street Farm next door to throw over the fire.

The base of the mill survived and a conical roof was placed over it. The business carried on with an oil-fired mill and John Pettit finally closed it in 1965.

The smock mill in a field next to Bridewell Lane, Botesdale.

This picture of the mill in Bridewell Lane is by Harry Hines. He was a landscape painter living in Botesdale in the early 20th century. The view is from the Gas House in Chapel Lane.

This photograph shows the post mill in Mill Road, Botesdale taken by Revd Farrer. It was situated where Miller's Orchard is today. The caption under Farrer's photo reads 'The mill alongside road leading to Botesdale Lodge quite demolished in 1924. The mill behind was Robinsons mill on Botesdale Green'. It is very difficult to see the mill on Botesdale Green that he refers to.

This is a very early drawing of a post mill in Mill Lane, Rickinghall. The image comes from a map of the land belonging to the church of Rickinghall Inferior in a 1791 church document.

There were several maltings in the villages. A huge one was situated where Jubilee House, Rickinghall stands today. This series of photographs shows it being demolished from 15th March 1926.

Before the demolition started.

The demolition was completed 1st May 1926.

Robinson Bros. were millers and merchants who owned several of the mills in the area and also the large maltings, where Jubilee House stands today, seen being demolished on the previous page. These two photographs show the Robinsons' warehouse which was between Hamblyn House and Walnut Tree Terrace. The warehouse was later demolished.

These two photographs show sacks being loaded onto carts from the warehouse in the early 20th century. The second photograph has a postage date of 1909.

This photo is of John Watts a harness maker.

An indenture survives from 7th October 1890 in which 12-year-old John Watts was apprenticed for four years to Edward Claydon of Botesdale who was a harness maker. Edward Claydon agreed to pay him one shilling a week for the first year, two shillings for the second year, three shillings for the third year and four shillings for the fourth year.

Horse collars can be seen behind the War Memorial. It is thought that this is where Edward Claydon had his business. It appears that Saddler Ray took over the workshop from him before moving across the Marketplace to the Old Saddlers.

The Old Saddlers with horse collars outside on the pavement.

Saddler Ray at the door of his workshop.

After Mr Ray had retired Alan Kerry, who repaired watches and clocks, had his workshop in this building. The photograph on the left shows the workshop in 1977.

The photograph on the right shows Alan Kerry in the doorway of his workshop.

James Horlick came to Botesdale in around 1900 and established his watch and clock making business in Honister House at this time. He

 was still in business in the late 1930s and died in 1943 when he was 80.

In the 18th century there were several clock makers in Botesdale. The ones we know about were William Shaw and his son, also William, George Shaw, Robert Brown and Christopher Bullock. Thomas Collins was working in the 19th century. We do not know exactly where their shops were but their clocks are still available.

This is a photo (left) of a clock made by William Shaw it was later completely restored by David Pratley, an expert horologist.

Robert Brown of Botesdale whose name appears on the clock above. Little is known about him although it is thought he was working in the early 18th century.

One of Thomas Collins' clocks.

In the 1830s and 1840s the Patrick family who lived in Forge Cottage, Rickinghall were blacksmiths, using the forge seen in this photograph. They were followed by the Warren family from the 1860s to the 1880s. Herbert Shemmings and later his son, Frank, were blacksmiths from the 1890s until the 1930s. Another son, Robert, died in WWI.

This photograph shows Forge Cottage, on the right, with Shemmings and the forge beyond it.

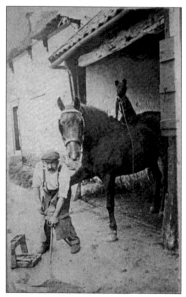

These two photos show Mr Frank Shemmings outside his forge.

E.J.Aves & Sons, builders. This business was started after WWII and by the 1960s was situated in Redgrave on the site which is now Redgrave Business Park. Aves were the builders used to construct the Botesdale Health Centre which opened in 1981.

The men in the lorry in the photograph above are, from left to right, Jack Edwards, Frank Gort, unknown, Wag Landymore.

F.C. Pemberton, Redgrave. This photograph was taken in 1977 at the time of the Queen's Jubilee, long after Frank Pemberton lived here. The white building on the left was originally his workshop and the

building in front of this was his shop. (See page 3). He described himself as a plumber, glazier, decorator and general contractor and lived in half of the house now known as Stagers.

He decorated the living room and passage at Victor Orves' garage in 1948 and priced 70 hours labour at £8.9s.6d. (£8.47½p). The total bill including materials was only £11.5s.3d. (£11.26p).

Mr Henry Bullock was a carpenter and general builder whose house and workshop was in The Street (almost opposite the former White Horse inn). Unwary visitors making their way through the house to the workshop might be surprised to see Mr Bullock screwing down the lid of a coffin - another service he provided was that of undertaker.

This photograph shows his workshop being restored. It became a private house now called Margaret Cottage.

One craftsman with a link to earlier times was Eric Burroughes who served an apprenticeship with P. W. Watson & Sons, coachbuilders of Diss. In 1923 he set up his business in a former chapel next to Southgate Farmhouse in Rickinghall where he built, painted and maintained carriages, carts and traps. Before long he had begun to adapt to the changing times and also

maintained and painted vans and buses. He was still working until the day before he died at the age of 80. This photograph shows the workshop in the old chapel.

Mr Burroughes in his workshop.

The heading from his invoice.

Hart family organ builders. This shed, in which organs were built, was situated in the garden of Walnut Tree House and Ivy Cottage (now called Rose Cottage).

Joseph Hart was an organ builder and built an organ for Redgrave Church in 1842 at a cost of £185. He was born in 1770 and died in 1856. His son Philip was also an organ builder. There are many organs built by Joseph Hart still in use in churches today.

A barrel organ (above) made by Joseph Hart.

Doe family thatchers. Graham Doe sitting outside his father John's house, Fairview in Redgrave. He came from a long line of thatchers dating back to 1694 when Samuel Doe thatched "Ye Fenn House". John later moved to Walnut Tree House as he wanted the old Hart organ builders' workshop to store his thatching materials and tools. John died in 1963 and his son Lancelot of Half Moon Lane carried on thatching until he retired.

Darcy Erith and his wife Ethel started a dairy farm at Ivy Farm in Redgrave in 1928, also delivering milk to the local community. They bottled the milk themselves and had bottles with their name on them. When they first started to deliver the milk Mrs Erith would deliver it by horse and cart. When he returned from the war in 1946 their son Lionel Robert (Bob) took over the milk delivery business. In 1953 he moved to Back Hills in Botesdale, and ran the business from there. When he retired in 1984 Turrells of Diss bought him out. Pearl Neave had by then taken over from him in Redgrave.

 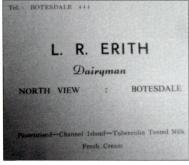

The first photograph is of Bob Erith's milk float on the day he retired, 24th February 1984. The second shows his business card.

Pearl Neave in October 1991. She retired in 1994.

Chapter 5
Inns and Public Houses

There have been many inns, pubs and alehouses in our villages through the ages. In the medieval period these were mostly alehouses. The earliest inn recorded in our villages' documents is The White Horse, Botesdale in the 14th century. In past centuries, before the time of radio or television, pubs and inns were the social hubs of the village where people, mostly men, could gather after work.

Redgrave

The Cross Keys is the oldest pub in Redgrave, probably dating back to the late 16th century. A rental of Redgrave Manor dated 1768 shows that Charles Simpson was the tenant and paid 4s. 6d. a year. In the 19th century it was in competition with two other pubs on the opposite side of The Knoll, The Fox and The Grapes. The Cross Keys became a community pub in November 2017. The date of this photo is unknown.

Frederick Grover, on the far right, was the landlord of The Cross Keys during WWII, when it was very busy with the American staff and patients from the hospital in nearby Redgrave Park. While Frederick's son Arthur was in the RAF, his wife Mildred and their son Brian lived at The Cross Keys.

The Cross Keys after the hurricane in 1987 when Michael Bishop was the landlord.

The Half Moon. This was another busy pub during WWII and has probably given its name to Half Moon Lane and Half Moon Green. It may have been a pub for over two hundred years. It is now a private house called Ash Tree Cottage.

Ash Tree Cottage formerly The Half Moon pub.

The Drum. This house on the edge of Redgrave Green, was a beer house. The footpath, leading from here to the market in Botesdale, is called Drum Lane on the enclosure map of 1818. The Drum was still open for business at the beginning of the 20th century.

Botesdale and Rickinghall

The Angel on Crown Hill. There was a public house called The Angel Inn from the 19th century until 1969. Like most village pubs it did not have a bar and customers ordered their drinks through a hatch. It is thought that this is the site of a 15th century alehouse. The present building dates from the early 18th century.

The Greyhound. The present Greyhound building dates from the late 15th century when it was an inn called The White Horse. It was first mentioned by name in a document dated 1503. By the late 18th century it had become The Greyhound and was a coaching inn. It was a stop on the route between London and Great Yarmouth and between London and Norwich.

Mr Frederick Williams with his wife and their daughter and son, Dudley, in the 1950s. Dudley later became the landlord, and held the tenancy until 2002.

This photograph of customers in the garden of The Greyhound pub probably dates to the 1920s. Jack Bryant is the young man standing in the centre, the man with the beard sitting next to him is his father Spenser Bryant. The others are not known but it is thought they were gamekeepers from the Redgrave Hall estate.

The Cock was situated where The Old Cock House, a private house, stands today. There was a pub on this site from at least the early 18th century when Thomas Slapp and his wife Sarah were the licensees. Like many pubs in the 20th century it had a darts team and the customers went on outings each year. In the early 20th century there was a barrel organ in the bar. This was exchanged for a jukebox in the 1950s for the benefit of the American servicemen who lived in the village at the time.

The Cock with bunting to celebrate the Coronation in June 1953.

An outing of The Cock's darts team in the 1930s. The man standing on the far right in the back row is Gordon Ray who was killed in WWII.

A summer outing in the late 1940s or early 1950s.
Back Row from left: John Garnham, unknown, Stanley Self, Wop Garnham, Bob Huggins, unknown, unknown, Cecil Wilby, George Bailey, unknown, Doris Wills, unknown, Alf Ramsey, Charlie Carver (landlord), Libby Self, unknown, Totty Orford, Bessie Lusby, Thora Smith, George Huggins, unknown, Frank Norman.
Front Row from left: Kenny Wilby, George Garnham, Peter Wilby, George Hawes, John Head, Tommy Bailey, unknown, ? Scarfe.

The Bell has probably been an inn since the early 17th century. In the 18th and early 19th centuries it was a coaching inn, where coaches stopped on their way between Cambridge and Great Yarmouth and Norwich and London. In WWII Tom Dunkley, whose wife's family had a circus, took over as landlord. At this time the circus animals were kept in the stables and fields behind the pub. Olga their daughter had a performing dog act.

The Bell in the early 20th century.

A photograph taken in 1977 with flags and bunting for the Queen's Silver Jubilee.

Olga Dunkley with her performing dogs outside The Bell.

In the 20th century, from the 1960s until the late 1990s, Hamblyn House was at various times an hotel, a restaurant and a country club.

An advertising postcard.

A page from the hotel brochure.

The first time The Golden Lion was described as a pub, with a brewery next to it, was in a document from 1855 when the owner was William Street. In 1897 it was sold to Tollemache's Brewery. Throughout the early 20th century it was a beer house and so could not sell spirits. It closed in the early 1960s and became a private house.

The photograph above on the right shows three girls, the middle one is Audrey Scott, outside the pub beside an army Jeep in the 1940s.

The photograph on the left shows Audrey Scott outside the pub, in 1944.

The building, which was formerly The White Horse inn can be traced back to the 17th century. It is possible that the business moved from the Marketplace in Botesdale in the early 19th century. The first reference we have to The White Horse where it is now is in 1825. It remained a pub until it closed in 2016 when it became a private house.

Three photos all taken in 1976. The sign changed from a galloping horse to a horse's head. At this time the pub was renovated and a porch was built on the front of the building.

Chapter 6
Churches and Chapels

It is likely that there were churches in Redgrave and Rickinghall from the Anglo-Saxon period. However three of the present churches date from the 11th to 14th centuries. In the 16th century, at the time of Edward VI, these became Protestant having been Roman Catholic until this time. In the 18th century non-conformism was very popular in East Anglia and by the 19th century we had many different dissenting chapels in our villages.

Redgrave

St Mary's Church, Redgrave. The present church building dates to the 14th century, although it is probably built on the site of the Saxon church mentioned in the Domesday Survey of 1086. It was built by the Abbot of the Benedictine Abbey of Bury St Edmunds. The tower was constructed of white brick in 1784 after the previous red brick tower blew down in a gale. It is famous for the monuments in the church.

St. Mary's Redgrave, taken from Hall Farm drive probably mid-20th century.

Sir Nicholas Bacon's monument (below). The base of this was carved by Bernard Jansen after the death of Lady Anne Bacon in 1616. After

Sir Nicholas' death in 1620, Nicholas Stone carved their white marble effigies on the top, one of which can be seen in this photograph.

Sir John Holt's monument in St. Mary's Church (right). He was Lord Chief Justice of The King's Bench and died in 1709.

121

As the church was a long way from the village and very cold in winter the Mission Room was built in 1897 for services to be held there when necessary. This photograph shows the Mission Room on its hundredth anniversary in 1997 after it had been refurbished.

Consecration of All Saints (formerly The Mission Room) on 7th September 2008. To the right of the Bishop, the Rt Revd Nigel Stock, is the Archdeacon the Ven Geoffrey Arrand and Revd Chris Norburn, Rector of Redgrave, Botesdale and Rickinghall.

The Methodist Chapel after its closure in 1994. It is now a private house.

Botesdale

Park View Chapel. Its predecessor The Gospel Hall was built around 1880. It was a wooden building which was brick-faced in the 1950s. This building was demolished and replaced by the present building in 1987 after which it became known as Park View Chapel. It was damaged by fire a couple of years later.

The old brick-faced building.

The new building as it was being finished.

It is likely that Botesdale Chapel of Ease, or St Botolph's Chapel as it was formerly known, was built as a market chapel in the late 13th or early 14th century. In the 15th century it became a chantry chapel where priests were paid to sing masses for the donor's soul. All chantries were dissolved in 1547, the first year of Edward VI's reign. The building was purchased by Sir Nicholas Bacon, lord of the manor, who founded a grammar school here in 1561. In 1883, after the school had closed, the building was bought by George Holt Wilson and became a chapel again with a board of trustees.

A drawing of the chapel from the early 19th century.

An early photograph probably also from the 19th century.

A slightly later photograph after the two trees had been removed. The inscription over the door of the chapel is to John Shreve and his wife, Juliana, who left money for it to become a chantry chapel.

Interior early 20th century (left).

The gallery decorated with flowers for a flower festival in 1969 (right).

The Wesleyan or Methodist Chapel was built in 1832. On the 6th January 1907 the building burnt down in under two hours. It had only recently been refurbished and an annex built for a Sunday school at a cost of nearly £200. It was rebuilt very soon afterwards with money raised by the congregation.

The building just after it had burnt down in 1907.

Workmen starting to rebuild it.

The chapel in 1977.

The building adjoining Southgate Farmhouse was once a Congregational Chapel built in about 1868.

St Mary's Rickinghall Inferior Church is a round tower church mentioned in the Domesday survey of 1086. The tower was built in the late 11th century and was heightened by an octagonal belfry in the 14th century. The chancel dates to the 13th century. The nave was enlarged by the addition of a south aisle and porch early in the 14th century and an upper chamber (or parvise) was added to the porch later that century. Much of the church was restored in the 1850s at the time of the Revd Maul.

The church in the early 20th century.

The church in the 1920s.

A view of the church from the crossroads.

Revd Hales with the Rickinghall Inferior church choir in front of the porch in the late 19th century.

Interior of the church in the early 20th century. Note the oil lamps then used to light the church.

The organ was still in the chancel at this time. It was later moved to its present position, at the west end of the nave.

Early Norman door in the tower on the first floor. At one time this probably had a ladder leading from the nave giving access to the tower.

St Mary's Rickinghall Superior Church dates from the 14th century, however the nave was rebuilt in the 15th century. The south porch with a parvise was added at this time. The stairs to the parvise and the stairs to the rood loft are still in place. The rood loft was the beam which went across the chancel arch, providing a walkway, so the rood, or cross, and candles could be reached. The stone seat running right around the inner wall of the nave was for the elderly and infirm as early medieval churches did not have pews. This gave rise to the expression 'the weakest go to the wall'. The church was made redundant in 1977 and taken over by the Redundant Churches Fund, now the Churches Conservation Trust, in 1980.

A view of the church taken in the early 20th century.

The north side of the church taken in the early 20th century when railings were still around the grave on the left.

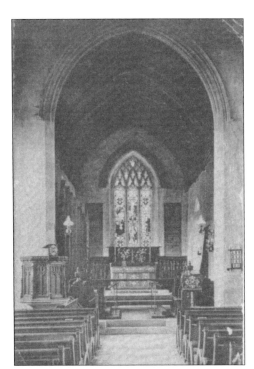

The interior of the church.

The re-hallowing service after restoration in 1962.

Chapter 7
Schools

There have been many schools in our villages in the past. Surviving documents show that as early as the 13th century, there was a school in Botesdale. In 1387 the documents mention that the village had a grammar school. By the late 18th century there were several private schools in all three villages. In the 1840s and 1850s National Schools were founded in both Redgrave and Rickinghall.

Redgrave and Botesdale National School, in Redgrave, was opened in 1845. It was instigated by the Rector, Revd T.D.H. Wilson and other parishioners and the land for the site was given by the Lord of the Manor, George St Vincent Wilson. All the children had to walk or cycle to school. Those from the far end of Fen Street in Redgrave travelled two to three miles; those from Botesdale slightly less.

Redgrave and Botesdale School with a postmark on the card of 1905. Notice the unmade road and the gap between the two buildings, before they were joined together when the school was expanded.

The headmaster in this photo is Mr William Henry Pursehouse who came to the school in 1893. He was a very popular headmaster who sadly died in 1907.

A school cycle outing to Knettishall Heath during WWII with teachers Mr and Mrs Hutchinson. Arthur Bryant is on the extreme left. He said it was the best day of his school life.

School dinners being served and eaten around the 1950s.

Children doing craftwork in the school also around the 1950s.

Redgrave and Botesdale School Christmas play 1948.

Christmas 1948.

Mrs Harvey and an infant class around 1955.

Infant teacher, Mrs Harvey, on retirement in July 1979. The headmaster is David Bristow.

Infant class playing percussion instruments in 1954-5.
From L to R: Back Row: unknown, unknown, Alva Garnham, Stewart Flatman.
Middle Row: Stewart Wilson, Derek Kempster, Gregory Rust, Jane Wilby, Linda Kemp, Jean Lister, unknown, Keith Flatman, unknown, unknown.
Front Row: Elved Harvey, Roger Walton, unknown, Gloria Stebbings, Jackie Erith, Rita Wilby, Sarah Williams, Bridgette Wilby, Dawn Harvey, Colin Ray, Christopher Whiting

Aerial view of Redgrave School showing a mobile classroom, a mobile office and the wooden canteen building. The canteen was introduced in 1942 and first used in January 1943.

The whole of Redgrave and Botesdale School in the last term of 1994. The man in the centre is Nigel Rhodes, the headmaster who became the first headmaster of a new school in Botesdale.

In September 1994 Redgrave and Botesdale School joined with Rickinghall's to form St. Botolph's Primary School in a new building in Botesdale. A newspaper photograph shows pupils gathered in the playground.

Sir Nicholas Bacon purchased the chapel building in Botesdale and in 1561 was granted permission by Queen Elizabeth to found a free grammar school in the building. Chapel House was built next door in 1571 to house the master and boarders. The building continued as a school until the mid-19th century.

Chapel building and Chapel House.

Back of the building in the 1920s.

A desk from the Grammar School covered with names and initials of the schoolboys over several generations. The desk is now in Redgrave Church. The boys also carved their names or initials into timbers in the Chapel House and the stone window lintels.

Mrs Taylor started a school in Botesdale after her husband died in 1877. For some years the school was in Osmond House but then in 1896 she moved to Chapel House, next door to the Chapel. This photograph shows some of her pupils in the back garden.

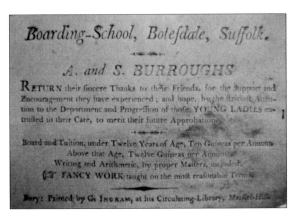

In the 18th and early 19th centuries Ann and Sarah Burroughs ran a boarding school for young ladies in Botesdale. They both drowned in a tragic boating accident at Orford in 1802. This card advertising their school was found recently behind a mantelpiece of a house in Redgrave.

The Dyer School. In 1825 John Dyer established a free school in Bridewell Lane in Botesdale for poor local children. After it was closed, in the 1860s, it was replaced by a purpose-built school in Fen Lane which opened in 1878. After this in turn closed in 1917 it eventually became a private house called The Old School House. This photograph shows the school before it was converted to a private residence.

Girls from the Dyer School in about 1915. Back Row: the girl third from the left is Barbara Horlick. Front Row: the girl third from the left is Nora Horlick. The others are unknown.

Photo of several children dressed as soldiers possibly at the time of the Boer War. The one little girl is dressed as a nurse. Unfortunately we do not know the names of any of the children in the photograph.

Olive and Muriel Warren's School was situated in two rooms of their home, Jubilee House in Rickinghall. They taught a small mixed school for boys and girls providing primary education from the early 1940s until the late 1950s.

This photograph shows the Misses Warren with their pupils in the garden of The Cottage (now The Old Vicarage) in July 1945 where they had gone on a school treat.

From L to R: Miss Muriel Warren, Jill Banham, Judy Smith, Michael Salt, Gareth Banham, Ann Goddard, Averil Anton, Ella Miles, Margaret Bryant, John Miles, Robert Reynolds, Miss Olive Warren Front Row: Eva Burrows, Robert Williams, Roger ?, Dorothy Goddard, Roland Bean, Janet Collins, Michael Flowerdew, Adrian Goddard.

Rickinghall National School was founded in the 1850s when the Revd Maul gave some of his glebe (church) land next to the churchyard. A building fund raised £650 to build the school and a two-storey schoolmaster's house.

Two early photographs of the church and school from The Street and Hinderclay Road.

The pupils gathered outside the school in the early 20th century.

The school in 1976.

Revd Hales and Mr Palmer, the headmaster, with the school 1902.

The school photograph from 1906.

Back Row: Walter Matthews, Gussie Crowe, Robert Bailey, Len Tipple, William Hayward, Percy Hayward, Gilbert Stebbing.

Fourth Row: Miss Burt, Sophie Whistlecraft, Maud Bailey, Ethel Pearce, ? Pearce, Pamela Stebbing, Lily Hayward, Dorothy Tipple, Jessie Matthews, Bertha Bailey.

Third Row: Adolphus Chenery, Arthur Smith, William Smith, Walter Garnham, Len Stebbing, Emma Gates, Ernie Whistlecraft, Harry Gates, Mr Palmer.

Second Row: Edith Bailey, Susan Bailey, Albert Crowe, Lily Pearce, Olive Garnham, Chris Stebbing, Elsie Bailey, Victor Reeve, Olive Smith.

Front Row: Oliver Chenery, Harold Miller, George Gates, William Gates, Arthur Fiske, John Ray.

On the back of this photograph is written 'Rickinghall School Hockey Team 1919'.
From L to R: Back Row: ? Bailey, Aggie Bullock, Nellie Sturgeon, Miss Helen Shemmings teacher, Doris Eater, Ivy Prentice, Hilda Wilmot.
Front Row: Rosie Baxter, Ruth Bailey, Roz Warren, Deborah Cook, Mary Baxter.

The boys from Rickinghall School were taken to this plot of ground, later called Little Patches, to learn gardening. The girls went to Stanwell House to learn how to cook and clean a house.

On the back of the photograph is written: 'October 1928. From left to right: Believed to be Joe Rice, Abi Banham, Stanley Perry. At the back near the hedge (school garden)'. Unfortunately we do not know who the other boys are.

Infants class photo from 1930. Peggy Healey (née Fellingham) was able to name all of the pupils.

From L to R: Back Row: John Hall, Monica Bloom, May Sparkes, Bertha Bailey, Daphne Foulger, Gladys Morley, Peggy Fellingham, Freddie Holden, Betty Noble, Charlie Self, Roland Ashford, Charlie Rush

Middle Row: Richie Cook, Barbara Buxton, Jean Ducker, Sylvia Stebbings, Irene Moule, Audrey Banham, June Banham, Edith Scoggins, Michael Foulger, Joan Harradine, Donald Macleod. Teacher: Mrs Phillips

Front Row: Iris Landymore, Joan Huggins, 'Snaps' Rush, Jimmy Moule, Kathleen Smith, Edith Bloomfield, Gordon Sterry, Ruby Bailey, 'Nobbler' Noble, Pearl Bailey, Amy Francis, Beryl 'Bonnie' Garnham

The Rickinghall School playing field in the mid-1950s. Tony Miller is the boy standing on one leg.

Rickinghall School just before it closed in 1994 with teachers and former pupils.

Chapter 8
Farming

In the medieval period agriculture was the mainstay of the local economy with the vast majority of people living off the land and depending on it to supply most of their needs. By the 17th century flax was being widely grown to make linen and farming employed increasing numbers of men and boys directly or as millers, blacksmiths, harness-makers and wheelwrights. Mechanisation in the mid-19th century began to reduce the number of workers needed and later the number of farms fell as land was amalgamated.

Redgrave

In the early 20th century the Boggis family had a business renting out various farm machines. Jack Boggis appears to have run this business in Redgrave from about 1915. These photographs show some of their machines. The photo on the left is of Benjamin and Harriet Boggis, who were Jack Boggis's parents. Note the shepherd's hut in the background.

A Boggis steam engine in Redgrave Park 1915.

Steam engine with members of the Boggis family, probably in Redgrave. Written on the photograph: 'Uncle Alfred Boggis, unknown, Jack Boggis (standing on the steam engine), unknown, Mr Sturgeon, Tom Boggis'.

Jack Boggis's threshing machine in action.

A steam threshing machine leaving the Boggis family yard on the junction of the road to Lopham and the Hinderclay road. A trade directory shows that Mrs Boggis owned the threshing machine in 1925.

Arthur Button built up his duck rearing business originally from his home in Redgrave Street, by cycling round locally buying ducks then plucking and selling them. After carrying on business at Sandhurst in Mill Lane, he developed his farm in Hinderclay Road, near Crackthorne Bridge. When the WWII American Hospital in Redgrave Park was dismantled Arthur bought the Nissen hut, which had been used as the operating theatre, to use on the farm. Arthur sold the business to Kerry Foods in 1990, who later sold to Gressingham Foods.

Ducks outside the factory in May 1968.

Factory flooded in September 1968.

Crackthorne Bridge in September 1968.

153

For 15 years George Ellinon plucked poultry for Arthur Button.

Arthur Musk bred ducks at Poultry Farmhouse, Fen Street, from at least 1911. This photograph, from the early 1920s, shows Fred Fellingham driving an ex-army lorry from WWI in the yard of the farm. The lorry had solid rear tyres and pneumatic tyres at the front.

There were two Street Farms in Redgrave Street. The one at the far end of The Street near Sandy Lane was bought by the Redgrave Estate in the 19th century. All the Estate Farms had enamel signs outside with their names on them. The farms were put on the market when the estate was sold in 1970. When postcodes were introduced one of the Street Farms had to change its name and Street Farm is now called Street Farm House.

During WWII Prisoners of War (POWs) from the camp in Redgrave Park worked on the local farms. This photograph shows two of them at Street Farm. From L to R is Ernst (POW), Kathleen Nunn, Wesley Nunn (farmer), Ruth Kronberger, (Jewish refugee), unknown (conscientious objector), Ralph (POW).

The other Street Farm in Redgrave Street had land which stretched to beyond Redgrave Church. This house was the farmhouse for Street Farm. In a marriage settlement of 1768 between John Rix Birch and Mary Jessop, the farm included a malt office, a malt kiln, mill house, barn, stables and other outhouses and buildings.

Ivy Farm, Redgrave Street. This farm was part of the Redgrave Estate and was known formerly as Butcher's Farm. It was let to D'arcy Erith from 1927 and in 1932 the rent was £110 a year plus repairs. This included the cottages which are now the Pink House and barn, on the opposite side of the road. D'arcy Erith's wife sold milk from the house and delivered it around Redgrave. The whole farm consisted of over one hundred and eighteen acres.

These photos show Ivy Farm Barn before and during conversion to three homes with an entrance to two more houses behind. The roof collapsed in 1984 and the building work was held up for a long time.

Hemp grown in the field along Hall Lane near the bridge between Redgrave and Botesdale. It was grown as a trial in 2011 for modern uses of hemp. In the past hemp was grown in Redgrave for linen weaving.

Written on the back of this photograph is: '1927. F. Sage Left 16 years Foreman. B. Foulger Middle. Taken when I was 14 years old. F. Garnham Right 16 years'. They appear to be sitting in front of reeds drying on a rack probably on Redgrave Fen.

This photograph shows Hedley and Harry Burroughes scything hay in the field behind Southgate Farmhouse in the 1920s. Their father owned the farm at this time. Their brother Eric later had his wheelwright business next door in the old Congregational Chapel.

Bringing in hay. Neither of the two men in this photo are known, nor is the horse.

George and Cliffy Bailey haymaking in 1974 on the field once called Accommodation Meadow. It is now called The Chestnuts and has houses built on it.

George Bailey with his horse Prince passing Church Farm, Rickinghall, after drilling sugar beet in the 1960s.

These pictures of haymaking at Rickinghall Inferior Rectory came from the Blyth family album. The photographs were taken around 1904. The young boys are the sons of Revd Blyth: William, Arthur and Reginald. Reginald died in the Battle of Jutland in 1916.

A painting by Mrs Blyth of haymaking in the field near The Rectory.

Making the hayrick.

The Blyth boys: William, Arthur and Reginald raking hay.

The Blyth boys on the back of the carthorse.

Snape Farm was the home farm for Hill House, now called Snape Hill House. Both were owned by the Norton family from 1842 until 1909 when the Holt Wilson family bought them. The Miles family have farmed Snape Farm since then, firstly as tenant farmers until they bought it in 1972.

A wagon in front of Snape Hill House in the early 20th century before the top storey and turret of the house were removed.

Charles Cook, who worked at the farm, with horse and cart. Snape Hill House can be seen in the background.

Charles Cook with a wagon in front of the cart shed which was blown down in the 1987 hurricane.

Ploughing, perhaps at Snape Farm, in the 1930s.

Harrowing on Clay Field between Calke Wood and the main road, in the 1930s.

Henry George Wilby, always known as George, reaping corn at Snape Farm. He is using a sail reaper which cut the corn, the three wooden sails then pushed it into lines. This was tied into sheaves by men following behind using rope made from the corn itself. This machine was superseded by the binder which automatically tied the corn into sheaves, a massive advancement.

William Cotton operating a threshing machine in a re-enactment in 1972.

Robert Cotton driving the steam engine.

An aerial view of Suggenhall Farm from the 1960s.

Two photographs of Kiln Farm and farmyard from a sales document of 1918.

Joe Rice and Ernie Whistlecraft working at Kiln Farm in the hamlet of Candle Street in the 1950s.

Tom Rush with a tractor in the 1930s. He worked at both Kiln Farm and Falcon's Hall. The family lived in a cottage belonging to Kiln Farm on Kiln Farm Lane.

West Hall Farm from across the fields.

West Hall Farmhouse from a sales document of 1918.

West Hall Farm outbuildings from the same 1918 sales document.

Robert Hall in front of the house in the 1930s.

This photograph, taken around 1926, is of John Robert Hall, his son Robert and grandson John Robert with a seed drill pulled by two horses. John Robert Hall bought the farm in 1919 and farmed it until he died in 1940 when his son Herbert took over. Herbert's grandson David Pettit now farms there.

Working at West Hall Farm taken in the 1930s. From L to R: Robert Hall, Ephraim Garnham, unknown, Bob Bailey and George Bailey (Bob's nephew).

Another photograph from about the same time. They are from L to R: Boney Hill, Fred Miller, unknown, unknown, Ephraim Garnham.

From L to R: Peter Cotton, Stanley Self and Derek Lummis with Darky the horse. In the 1950s.

Corn stooks in Chubbins Field, West Hall Farm, looking towards Jackamans Farm. Six sheaves make up a stook, called a shock in Suffolk.

Charlie Rush on a Nuffield tractor with Fred Miller behind, hoeing sugar beet. This tractor used petrol and paraffin.

David Pettit combining wheat in Chubbins Field, West Hall Farm in 2016.

Unloading grain at midnight 2016.

Stone Hall in the 1960s.

A poor photograph of working horses being taken along Back Hills.

Bury St Edmunds sheep market in the 1950s. William George Harvey is driving the sheep towards the camera. He owned Harveys' haulage business in Rickinghall.

Alfred 'Wop' Garnham, seen here with a fox cub, left school at the age of 13½ and in 1919 went to work as a gamekeeper for Lord Playfair who was renting the Redgrave Estate at the time. He worked there until the war years and afterwards returned as head keeper from the 1950s until the 1970s. He lived at the Water House in Redgrave Park then moved to a bungalow in Mill Lane, Rickinghall with his partner Betty Squirrel, herself a gamekeeper.

Joe Whistlecraft was a poacher who turned gamekeeper.

This photo shows Harry Ray, who was born in 1868, sharpening his scythe with a whetstone. The photograph was taken in the 1930s. In his younger days he was often arrested for poaching and once for playing pitch-and-toss on a Sunday!

Frederick Cook in front of Rickinghall Superior Church porch in the 1930s. He was sexton and used a scythe to cut the grass in the churchyard.

Chapter 9
People

This chapter is about the people and families who have lived or are still living in Botesdale, Redgrave and Rickinghall. A large number of people have kindly given us their family photographs and we have put in as many as possible. The people they show range from bright-eyed, young schoolchildren to the very elderly whose formal, serious poses reflect the essence of the Victorian or Edwardian periods to which they belonged.

Many of those photographed are no longer with us; for some, their names will bring back memories: Arthur Bryant, Basil Brown, Denis and Audrey Simonds, Mr and Mrs Sage, Dr Richardson, Nurse Farnish and Margaret Gowan. There are one or two striking images: a beautifully composed photograph of Albert Driver and an extraordinary image of Bob Ray on a tightrope.

The Sunday School at Rickinghall Inferior Church in the 1950s. From L to R: Back Row: Harry Bullock, Portland Bailey, Derek Foulger, Colin Arnold, Mrs Flowerdew, unknown, Mrs Payne.

Front Row: Kevin Bailey, Sandra Arnold, Marcia Healey, Susan Bailey, Christine Seeley, Unknown, Sally Bailey.

Visit of a Malaysian Princess outside The Cottage, Redgrave, 1965.

From L to R: Back Row: Mrs Haywood, Unknown, Mrs Banham, Susan Orr. Middle Row: Gladys Rain, Annette Orr, the Malaysian Princess, Elsie Young, Daphne Culley, Scipia Hawes. Stewart Orr kneeling in the front.

Planting a tree in front of the Methodist Chapel in Redgrave, with church members in attendance, to celebrate the Golden Jubilee of the Women's Institute in 1965. Another tree was planted outside the Mission Room. From L to R: Mrs. Driver, Madge True, Mrs Banham, Mrs Hudson, Daphne Culley, Margaret Kemp, Mrs Cater, Kathleen Reeder, Millie Flatman (president), Walter Cater, Elsie Young (with spade), Scipia Hawes. Claire Kemp is the little girl at front.

James Reeder Bailey's wedding to Jean Fulcher took place on 12th June 1948. In the spring of 1949 they re-enacted their wedding for 'Village in the Wheatfields' a film about life in the country produced by The Central Office of Information.

The bridal party, James Reeder Bailey and Jean Fulcher with their bridesmaids Joyce Fulcher, Wendy Williams and Doreen Bailey.

Sarah Bailey, née Plume, with daughter Kate Albina Self née Bailey and granddaughter Esther Self, taken around 1915. Sarah and James Reeder Bailey senior were grandparents of Frederick Bailey and great grandparents of James Reeder Bailey.

Wedding of Agnes Bailey to Frederick Francis on 21st October 1914.

L to R: Back Row: Edgar Bailey, James Reeder Bailey senior, Arthur Charles Bailey, William Francis, Charles Edgar Markham, Maud Bailey. (Arthur Bailey and Charles Markham, fiancé of Maud, were both killed in WWI.)

Front Row: Mr & Mrs Alfred Francis parents of groom, Mabel Francis, Frederick Francis groom, Agnes Bailey bride, Jane Bailey mother of bride, Helen Bailey bride's daughter, Henry Bailey bride's father.

The wedding of Maud Bailey and Sidney Kettley in the Summer of 1931.

From L to R: Back Row: 3rd from left Frederick Bailey bride's brother, 5th from left Herbert Bailey bride's father.

Front Row: 3rd from left Mary Bailey bridesmaid and sister of the bride, Sidney Kettley groom, Maud Bailey bride, Ellen Bailey mother of the bride.

Frederick Bailey with his sister Susie (right).

Tip Hayward with Herbert Bailey (left).

This photograph is of the wedding of Jack Boggis who had a machinery business in Redgrave from about 1915 until the late 1920s. (See page 150). The couple on the right are his brother Arthur and his wife Lottie. Unfortunately we do not know the name of Jack's wife.

Basil Brown was the archaeologist who discovered the Sutton Hoo ship burial in 1939. Although self-taught he was a highly skilled archaeologist and carried out many excavations around our villages.

This photo shows Basil with a piece of Roman Samian ware pottery outside the shed in his garden. This shed contained a large collection of archaeological finds.

A photo from Basil's own album showing him at the excavation he did at Cooks Field in Garden House Lane.

Arthur Bryant aged about six. (See page 41).

This photo shows Arthur with his brother Ken on a cycle holiday in Yorkshire. For many years they worked as local builders known as the Bryant Bros.

Eliza Burroughes who lived at Southgate Farmhouse in the early part of the 20th century. Her son Eric was the coachbuilder and wheelwright whose workshop was in the old Congregational Chapel next door.

This photo is of Arthur Chilvers, taken in WWI. He had a shop in the Chilvers building in the Marketplace which he and his wife Bessie started in the 1930s. His son Kenneth took it over with his wife Mary. It finally closed in the 1980s. (See page 72).

This photo taken just before WWI is of the servants of the Gascoigne family at Henley Hall near Ipswich. Eva Cook, in uniform on the left, grew up in Rickinghall and was in service all her life with the family as their cook. When the family moved to South Kensington she and Miss Crosby, on the right, the lady's maid went too.

Albert Driver in 2008 aged 93. This was the 80th time he had rung the bells for Harvest Festival at Redgrave Church. He was presented with honorary life membership of the Suffolk Guild of Ringers. When Albert became tower captain in 1939 following the death of his father, he was the third successive generation of his family to hold the post.

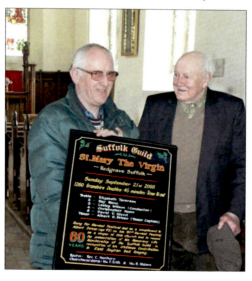

Revd Edmund Farrer was born in 1848 to a wealthy family near Swaffham in Norfolk. In 1878 he was ordained, became Curate of Rickinghall Inferior in 1890 then Rector of Hinderclay until he retired in 1915. He was an enthusiastic antiquary and photographer.

Nurse Alice Farnish was the district nurse and midwife for the area for 34 years. She started work in November 1929 and retired in 1963. In that time she delivered over 1,000 babies.

This photograph shows Nurse Farnish holding the 1,000th baby she delivered, Sarah Green of Redgrave. Farnish House, the sheltered housing complex in Botesdale, is named after her.

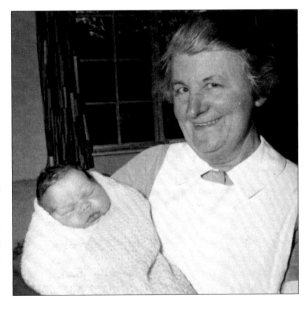

Peggy Fellingham whose mother, Rosetta, kept the shop at Chestnut view. (See page 90).

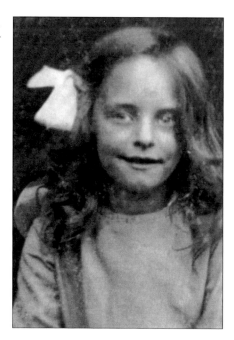

Peggy in her Royal Observer Corps uniform during WWII. She served from the age of 18 in 1941 and would spend several shifts a week in the Observer Post on Botesdale Common.

Jim Healey, who was later to become Peggy's husband, worked at Prisoner of War Camp 56 in Botesdale from 1945. There were several social events at the camp and he met Peggy at a dance there. Peggy checked his pay book to make sure he wasn't married! Jim and Peggy were married in 1947.

Peggy's father, Fred Fellingham, in his Royal Observer Corps uniform in 1956.

The Gooderham family farmed at Church Farm, Rickinghall for many years from the early 19th century. When George William Gooderham died in 1916 the family moved to Diss.

George William and his wife Mary Ann in August 1868.

The family outside Church Farm, Rickinghall. From L to R: Back Row: Mary, Tom Fitt, Dolly (Helen), George White, Annie. Front Row: Evelyn Gooderham, Olive, George William Gooderham.

Charles Gosling was the Police Constable for Botesdale during WWII. This photograph shows him with Sgt. Smith of the USAF with whom he liaised.

The Gowen family came to Botesdale in the late 1940s and soon afterwards Margaret Gowen opened the 'Copper Kettle' tea rooms at their home, Osmond House. She ran the annual Quality Fair from 1964 to 1989, raising money for charity. She also held a luncheon club in her house for pensioners. In 1990 she was awarded the British Empire Medal for services to the community. This photograph shows Sir Joshua Rowley, Bt., Lord Lieutenant of Suffolk, presenting her with the award.

The Revd Hales with his second wife, family and servants outside The Rectory, Rickinghall Inferior. He was Rector of Rickinghall Inferior from 1889 until 1902.

A photograph of Doctor Maurice Hannigan, his wife and two daughters in the 1930s outside their house, The Priory, where he also had his surgery. He bought the practice and house from the previous doctor, Dr Pearse, in 1897 and continued there until the mid-1930s when Dr Ward became the medical practitioner.

This photo is of John Robert Hall, his wife Elizabeth and their children. It was probably taken in 1915 when their son Robert came home after being injured in the war.
From L to R: Back Row: Isobel, Robert, Mary.
Middle Row seated: John Hector, John Robert and Elizabeth, William.
Front Row: Kathleen, Herbert.

The wedding of Isobel Hall and Frederick Barker took place on 15th June 1922
From L to R: Front Row: Herbert Hall, Mr & Mrs F W Barker bridegroom's parents, Edith Barker, bride and groom, Kathy Hall, Elizabeth and John Hall the bride's parents.

The wedding of James William Harvey to Maud Mary Boyce in December 1899 (right). He was 24 years old and she was 18. They lived in Church Farm next to Chapel House in Botesdale. Their son Henry and his wife Phyllis lived in St Catherines in Botesdale. They are the grandparents of Peter Harvey, Dawn Hall and Hilary Townsend née Harvey.

Sarah Harvey née Flatt mother of James William Harvey.

Sarah's husband James Harvey father of James William Harvey.

The Halsted family lived at Brook House from 1902 until Col John Ord Halsted died in 1916. This photograph shows them outside Brook House. Col Halsted is sitting in the middle with his wife, Eliza, in the white bonnet next to him. One of their daughters Violet Halsted, who was recognised as a minor Suffolk artist, is on the back row fourth from the left.

Violet Annie Horsfall lived at Redgrave Hall, which her husband rented from George Holt Wilson between 1895 and 1898. She bred Great Danes and was also a judge for the Great Dane Club, and an associate of The Kennel Club.

The Huggins family. The wedding of Stanley Huggins to Hilda Souter on 17th September 1938 at Rickinghall Superior Church.

The wedding of Margaret Huggins and Terry Andrews at Redgrave Church in 1965.
From L to R: Terry Andrew's foster mother, Bertram and Ethel Huggins parents of the bride, Greta and John Huggins, Florence Huggins widow of Bert Huggins who was killed in WWI and mother of Bertram, Joan and George, the groom and bride. Next to them, the bridesmaids Pamela Huggins and in front of her are her sisters Linda and Jill daughters of John, partially hidden is Paula Huggins sister of the bride. At the back are Jack Clears and his wife Joan née Huggins, George and Thora Huggins.

Mr and Mrs Kerry in their newsagents shop, next to The Bell Inn, in Rickinghall.

Lenny Prentice who lived at Fairhaven in Botesdale, opposite Simonds Court. His brother Victor was killed in WWI.

Charles Norton, the son of Thomas Norton a chemist from Beccles, bought Snape Hill House, then called Hill House, with Snape Farm from John Amys in 1842. He married Louisa Nunn a girl from the village and they had 11 children.

A painting of Thomas Norton with his son Charles in the 1820s.

Wedding photograph of Archibald Lacy-Scott and Helen Norton, one of Charles and Louisa's children, in 1902 in front of Hill House.

Photo of many of the family taken in 1909 outside Hill House.
From L to R: Back Row: Charles Norton junior, Louisa Norton née Nunn mother, Lancelot Hale, Revd William Aldred, Sophie Norton.
Front Row: Helen and Archibald Lacy-Scott, Harriet Hale née Norton with Rosalie, Ellen Aldred née Norton with Dorothy, Revd Victor Norton, Janet Norton.

Louisa Nunn with her daughters outside Hill House 1909 just before it was sold.
From L to R: Sophie, Harriet, Helen, Louisa, Janet, Ethel.

Wedding of Victor and Miriam Orves in 1917. Victor was Lord Playfair's chauffeur and Miriam was Lady Playfair's maid. Victor later started his cycle business and garage in Redgrave.

Victor at the wheel of Lord Playfair's car.

Victor's son Dudley was born in 1928 and baptised in Redgrave church by a bishop. Dudley worked at the garage and carried on his father's business after Victor retired in 1957. Dudley died in 2003 and left his estate divided between Redgrave Church, the Health Centre and Addenbrooke's Hospital

A photo of Dudley as a young man.

Mr & Mrs Pettit, from the mill at Redgrave, on a day out in Hunstanton about 1938. Lionel Erith is at the back and Edward Parish is on the right. Edward was killed in 1941 in WWII.

Hon Lyon Playfair was the son of Lord and Lady Playfair who lived at Redgrave Hall. He was killed in WWI in 1915 and there is a stained glass window in Redgrave Church in memory of him.

Wesley Ray, along with his younger brother Bob, his elder brother Jack and a friend 'Tiny' Goddard formed a tightrope and balancing act called The Atlas Brothers or sometimes The Ray Brothers. They performed with Rosaire's Circus before WWII around East Anglia and at local fetes and shows.

Wesley and Bob practising.

Tiny Goddard supporting Bob.

Performing at a fete in Rickinghall. The Dyer School in Fen Lane can be seen in the background.

Bob on a tightrope at the circus (below).

Isabella Miller whose two sons, Frederick and James died in WWI. Her daughter Hilda married Tom Rush.

Tom Rush and his wife Hilda with Jean their daughter. Tom was in the regular army in the 1st Battalion Suffolk Regiment. He was taken prisoner in 1915. He spent much of his time as a Prisoner of War working on a farm in the Netherlands. After the war he worked at Kiln Farm in Candle Street.

Tom Rush with their children Ivy, Rosie, Jean and Ken.

Dr David Ryder Richardson was a doctor in the village for 33 years. He retired in 1985. Before the Medical Centre was built the surgery was in his house, The Homestead in Rickinghall. Ryders Way in Rickinghall is named after him. This photo was taken in 1985 in the garden of his home with his wife Sonia.

Francis and Doris Sage taken in their fish & chip shop in the Marketplace. The business is still in the same family with their grandson Richard Lewis now running it.

This is a photograph taken outside the Methodist Chapel after a service to celebrate Miss Ethel Scates' 80th birthday in 1955. For many years she ran a private school at her home, Mowbray House. Her mother helped to raise the money to rebuild the Methodist Chapel after the fire in 1907. (See page 126).

An enlargement from another photograph taken on the same day.

Rowland (Ossie) Simonds started his bus company in the 1930s in Botesdale. After his death in the 1970s his children Jean, Audrey and Denis ran the business. In 2004 the business relocated to Diss. (See page 68).

Ossie Simonds

Ossie and Rosalind's children Jean, Denis and Audrey.

Jean Bennett née Simonds.

Audrey Simonds.

Samuel Speare was a village boy from Rickinghall who in 1868, at the age of 15, went out to Zanzibar as a missionary. He stayed there for five years returning in August 1873. He died at the age of 20 at Burgh le Marsh in Lincolnshire on 11th November 1873 where he was being prepared to be ordained. He is commemorated in a window in Rickinghall Superior Church.

Paul Stobbe was a German pilot who was shot down in 1940 when he was about 20. He was brought to West Hall Farm from the POW camp at Botesdale to work on the land and was billeted in the farmhouse. He stayed on after the war and worked for the Hall family at West Hall Farm for about 30 years. He was granted UK citizenship in 1965. He was a good footballer mainly playing in goal for Rickinghall, later becoming a referee. He died in 1973 at the age of 53.

The Watts family of Redgrave. John Watts, harness maker, third from left at the back. (See page 100).

Elizabeth Horlick (right) wife of James Horlick the clock maker (See page 98), mother of five daughters Barbara, Nora, Miriam, Doris and Beatrice.

Beryl Churchyard née Wilby (left) and Adrian in the 1930s, two of Beatrice's children, grandchildren of James and Elizabeth.

The wedding of Ernie Baxter and Mary Wilby (no relation to the Wilby family mentioned previously) on 14th March 1959 at the Methodist Chapel.

Mary and Ernie on their 60th wedding anniversary at the Methodist Chapel 16th March 2019.

Mary's grandfather and grandmother, George and Eliza Wilby at Potters Farm in about 1900. The photograph shows them with their eldest daughters from L to R: Jessie on George's knee, Rose sitting in front, Nancy on Eliza's knee and Maria. They had eight daughters and two sons.

Helen Wilby, Mary's mother, on the right with Sophie Whistlecraft on the left.

Lucy and George Holt Wilson in 1877 with eight of their ten children.

Lucy Wilson with two of her children in a pram (above).

Lucy Wilson probably holding her eldest son, George Rowland Holt Wilson (right).

Arthur Woodrow joined the Royal Worcestershire Regiment. His father was in the home guard.

The Woodrow family outside Birds Cottage, Half Moon Lane, Redgrave in 1941.

The Revd Blyth came to Rickinghall in 1903 from Wetheringsett and was the Rector here until 1913 when he died. The family had several photograph albums from this time. Many of the photographs are of the family but there are also several of village people. Sadly we do not know any of the names of these villagers.

The Blyth children in the early 20th century From L to R: William, Arthur, Margaret (Margie) and Reginald (Reggie).

The Blyth family From L to R: Reggie, Arthur, Margie, William, Revd Cecil and Mrs Annie Blyth with Tuppence the dog.

Rickinghall Rectory. From L to R: Reggie, William, Margie, Arthur, and Tuppence the dog.

Reggie was a career naval officer becoming a Lieutenant in 1913. He was killed in 1916 at the Battle of Jutland.

Revd Cecil Blyth with his tame doves outside The Rectory, Rickinghall Inferior.

These two photos are of a group of young girls with Revd Blyth's wife, centre back row. In the first photograph they are looking at a photograph album.

A group of old ladies, young ladies and little girls in front of The Rectory with Mrs Blyth.

A group of village ladies with the family maids and Tuppence the dog. Mrs Blyth is third from the left centre row.

A group of young girls with their needlework in front of The Rectory. Is this a sewing class?

Two delightful photographs of some of the elderly ladies from the village. Mrs Blyth and her daughter Margie are standing at the back in the top photo.

Chapter 10
Special Occasions

On certain special occasions, such as Queen Elizabeth's Coronation, the villages would celebrate with a festival or ceremony with events taking place over one or two days. Photographs were also taken of such things as the opening of the bypass and of the first housing estate being built on the Fairstead in Botesdale.

A fair had been held in Botesdale for many years in the medieval period on the eve and day of St Botolph, 17th June. In the 19th century a fair was held annually on Ascension Day but this was abolished in 1873. In the 20th century a yearly funfair came to Botesdale.

The ceremony to unveil the War Memorial took place on Sunday 8th August 1920. In the presence of over 2,000 people it was unveiled by Brigadier General Lord Playfair, whose son Lyon had been killed on active service in 1915. The memorial was dedicated by Revd L.H. Wilson.

Many clubs, businesses and pubs arranged outings for their members each year. In the days when few people owned cars, this brought together groups of like-minded people to enjoy a day out together.

A charabanc outing in the early 1920s. We do not know where they were going but they seem to be enjoying their day out!

An outing of E.J. Aves, builders, in the early 1950s. From L to R: Back Row: Bud Aves, ? Cotton.
Front Row: Walter Erith, David Aves, Henry Harvey, Jim Healey, Bert Wilby.

This photograph shows the children of Botesdale celebrating King George V's Silver Jubilee which took place in May 1935. They are gathered in front of the pavilion on Barley Birch, the playing field opposite the Toll House in Botesdale. The pavilion was later moved to Rickinghall playing field on a low loader.

We have only been able to identify a few of these children.

From L to R: Second Row: 5th Jean Bennett née Simonds, 7th Joan Cook née Wilby, 11th Audrey Simonds.

Front Row: 1st Joan Garnham, 6th Harold Gurdon, 9th Denis Simonds, 11th Arthur Bryant.

These photographs show the celebrations of the Coronation of Queen Elizabeth II in June 1953.

This photograph was probably taken the day before when several people dressed up to advertise the event. It is not certain who the people are but it is thought that the sailor is Basil Orford, the girl in the frilly dress is Sheila Parry, the clown is possibly Flora Smith, the man with bowler hat is probably George Garnham and the girl at the back right Molly Mills née Kemp,

The procession on the way to Rickinghall sports field passing what is now Chestnut View.

The procession passing Pound Farm barn. Fred Fellingham junior and Fred Fellingham senior are pulling Jim Healey in HMS Rickinghall.

Jim Healey in HMS Rickinghall.

Jim Healey in HMS Rickinghall on the playing field in Rickinghall.

Another decorated cart with a group of children in fancy dress. The girl at the front appears to be dressed as Britannia. It is not known who these children are.

From L to R: Elizabeth Compton, Paul and Portland Bailey (the bride and groom), Marguerite Payne, Alison Compton, Jean Compton.

The same float at the playing field. From L to R: Alison and Jean Compton, Marguerite Payne, Paul and Portland Bailey. Jim Bailey, father of Paul and Portland, standing beside the float with Eileen Payne, mother of Marguerite next to him.

Redgrave and Botesdale School's May Day celebrations in 1972 featuring Tracy Sharp as May Queen. The float and children visited Botesdale in the morning and Redgrave Knoll in the afternoon, distributing paper flowers to the villagers who came to see the children dancing. Both these photographs were taken outside the Cross Keys pub.

Donna Taylor as the Fete Queen at the Redgrave cum Botesdale Church Fete in the 1970s.

Claire Shepherd chosen as 'Miss Redgrave' for the 1975 Redgrave Festival. The two attendants were Anne Newman on Claire's right and Donna Taylor on her left.

These photographs show the festival to celebrate the Queen's Silver Jubilee held from the 4th to the 7th June 1977.

MONDAY JUNE 6th

&

TUESDAY JUNE 7th

AT BOTESDALE CHURCH ROOM

FLOWER, VEGETABLE & PRODUCE SHOW
(All Entries between 9 a.m. & 10 a.m. Monday)

ARTS & CRAFTS EXHIBITION
(All entries Saturday or Sunday 2 to 4 p.m.)

OPEN MONDAY 2 to 6 p.m.
OPEN TUESDAY 10 a.m. to 6 p.m.

Entrance 5p

* * * * *

ROUNDHOUSE OPEN

FOR

DISPLAY OF MURALS

* * * * *

WHEELWRIGHTS DISPLAY

AT Mr. E. BURROUGHES

* * * * *

BEST DECORATED HOUSE IN VILLAGE
TO BE JUDGED ON MONDAY

The programme for the festivities.

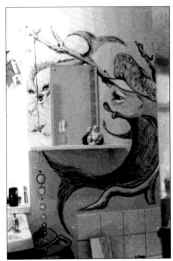

The Roundhouse, now called The Toll House, was open for people to view the mural display.

The Royal British Legion float passing St Catherines. The lady standing at the gate is Elizabeth Craig, the cookery writer.

The Playgroup float.

The Gospel Hall Sunday School float 'HMS Royal Ark'. This float won first prize.

The Royal Yacht Britannia float passing Last's butchers shop. This float made by the Bryant Bros. won third prize.

The Rickinghall Women's Institute float 'The Worzel' won second prize.

The Women's Institute float. From L to R: Pat Moynihan, possibly Cynthia Powell, Rosie Cox, Betty Mayhew, Maggie Wilson and Nellie Wilson.

Botesdale Wives Club float. From L to R: Mary Baxter, Barbara Rice, Pam Foulger, Marjorie Cotton, Diana Sturgeon. On the other side were Ann Catlin, Margaret Andrew, Beryl Hill, Mrs Bracewell, Mrs Bradshaw.

The Fairstead housing estate being built in 1988. The common land of The Fairstead was sold to a developer to build houses.

In the 1920s Dr Barnardos children were sent to families in our villages to be fostered. Patty Thompson fostered two children Florrie Hinton (then called Nora Thorne) and Lily Gardiner. After living as sisters for seven years Florrie was sent to Western Australia in 1932 and Lily went back to the Dr Barnardos home at Barkingside. In 1981 Florrie visited England and a reunion was organised with Lily Gardiner and many of the people who had known the girls when they lived in Redgrave.

L to R: Back Row: Barbara Rice née Baxter, Bernard Fisher, Cecil Wilby, Jimmy Harvey, Annie Cross née Markell.
Middle Row: Millie Sharman, Lily Greenhill née Gardiner, Sheila Sturgeon, Verona Fisher, Lillian Lummis.
Front Row: Elsie Buxton, Florrie Hinton, Millie Flatman née Musk. Elsie Buxton and Millie Flatman were the teachers at Redgrave and Botesdale School who taught the girls.

Florrie and Lily were shown round the house, now Charity Cottage, where they lived with Patty Thompson, by Don and Joan Day, the new owners.

In 1991 The Heritage Circle organised a reunion for children evacuated to the villages during World War II. Seen here at Rickinghall Village Hall, the evacuees were able to visit their old schools and some of the houses where evacuees were fostered.

Redgrave Fen. David Bellamy, conservationist, helping to launch the restoration of Redgrave and Lopham Fen in July 1995. The fen had been drying out after a borehole had been dug to supply local villages with water. David had studied the flora and fauna on the fen in 1959 for his degree and knew the changes which water extraction had made.

The site was declared a National Nature Reserve in 1993 when it was the only known site where the rare great raft spider was found. More sites have since been discovered. The European Union pledged £1.4 million towards the £3.2 million needed for the project.

Another part of the project was to import wild Polish Konik ponies to help to clear the scrub. These small horses thrive in the wetland areas of Poland. Originally four mares in foal and one stallion were brought to Redgrave and Lopham Fen in 1995; now their descendants have been introduced to other nature reserves.

The Konik ponies are very inquisitive and came to inspect the firemen and engine when fire broke out in 1996. The fireman is Jonathan Wilby. Fires were a common occurrence in summer when the fen was very dry but now the water is back this does not happen.

239

Prince Charles visiting Redgrave Church in 1993 as patron of the charity 'Music in Country Churches'. He landed by helicopter in Redgrave Park where he was met by the Lord Lieutenant of Suffolk, Sir Joshua Rowley, before being driven to the church.

Fifty children from Redgrave School walked from the school to the church to meet Prince Charles. They presented him with two school T-shirts for his sons Princes William and Harry.

One of the most dramatic changes for Botesdale and Rickinghall began in the late 1980s with the suggestion of a bypass to relieve congestion in The Street. A formal notice of the planning application was posted near the proposed route of the bypass. The road behind was the main road. It is now the lane going up to the bottle bank and Snape Farm.

Before and after photographs of the road going past Briar Lane, which leads to West Street.

A view of the road being started.

Before and after photographs of the road cutting through Jacobites Wood.

An underpass was built so that riders on horseback using Bridewell Lane could go under the bypass.

The bypass being opened by Jeffrey Stansfield, Chief Highways Engineer, on 11th November 1995.

The Rickinghall Silver Band outside The Cottage (now The Old Vicarage) in Rickinghall in the early 20th century.

The band outside Jessamine House in Rickinghall at a similar date.

The band in about 1912. The boy on the left is Wesley Ray.

The band playing at a fete, possibly in Rickinghall.

An early photograph of the band taken in about 1908.

From L to R: Back Row: H Bailey, G Woods, F Bailey, W Elliot, R Woods, F Wilby.
Middle Row: D Lummis, F Francis, A Chenery, H Shemming, R Baxter, C Kemp (Band Master).
Front Row: E Tuffs, F Smith, D Kemp, J Bailey, W Lummis.

The Rickinghall Silver Band in 1933. They are from L to R:
Back Row: Fred Bailey, S Bullock, Arthur Francis, Leslie Kemp, Unknown.
Middle Row: Tom Shaw, Jack Cotton, Unknown, Unknown, A Chenery, Unknown, R Cotton.
Front Row: William Cotton, G Baxter, Herman Moule, Fred Francis (Band Master), Tom Bailey, Ronnie Francis, Robert Baxter.

The dedication of the Rickinghall Women's Institute Banner, which had been made by several of the members, in August 1954. Mrs Flowerdew, who lived in The Cottage, is holding the banner pole. Gladys Tuck, who lived at Brook House, is on her left. Her sisters Sybyl and Hylda Tuck are standing directly behind Mrs Flowerdew. Pleasance Warren is on her right.

This tapestry was made to celebrate the Millennium. Several clubs and groups each made squares and these were sewn together to form the banner.

Chapter 11
Sports

The previous two chapters have shown how village communities are drawn together by family gatherings like weddings and by national occasions such as royal events. Various different sports also bring people together and have been an important part of village life through the ages. Camping, a type of football, was played in the middle ages. There were horse races at Barley Birch in Botesdale in the 19th century and point-to-point events took place from Allwood Green to Botesdale.

Cricket was very popular; however football appears to have been the main leisure occupation for the young men of the village. It was played in the schools but the villages had teams taking part in leagues, such as the Eye and District League. Hockey was played by the girls at school and in the 1930s shinty, a game like hockey, was introduced. In the 20th century bowls became popular while most pubs had their own darts teams.

A photograph of Rickinghall School football team in 1924. Unfortunately we only have the name of one of the boys, Alfie Ray the boy holding the ball.

The school team in 1925. Again we only know Alfie Ray. In this photograph, he still has the ball.

Rickinghall School football team 1933-34.

Rickinghall School football team 1952-53.

From L to R: Back Row: F.L.G. Reynolds the headmaster, Derek Lummis, Denny Peters, ? Montgomery, David Pettit, Winston Canham. Front Row: Terry Collins, Unknown, Tony Chillistone, Joe Goldman, Gareth Banham, unknown.

Rickinghall School team 1954-55. The headmaster F.L.G. Reynolds standing at the back.
From L to R: Back Row: Gerald Canham, David Woodward, Edward Thorold, Bernard Mullinger, Cedric Snowling, Robin Davey, Christopher Sturgeon, Willie Arnold.
Front Row: Roy Peters, George Garnham (Sonny), Derek Lummis, Tony Chillistone, Winston Canham, Aubrey Seeley, David Pettit.

Rickinghall football team played in the Eye and District League. They won the league cup four years running from 1948 to 1951.

L to R: Back Row: Fred Miller, Jimmy Bailey, Jack Kemp, Unknown, Ronnie Francis, Noel Foulger. Front Row: Stanley Miller, Derek Harvey, Alfie Ray, Ronnie Farrow, Francis Chillistone.

From L to R: Back Row: Paul Stobbe, Ron Francis, Albert Hill, Derek Harvey, Jack Kemp, Noel Foulger, A Legget, T Holden, J Miller.
Front Row: Francis Chillistone, Peter Cotton, Alfie Ray, Ronnie Farrow, Stanley Miller.

From L to R: Back Row: Joe Goldman, Gordon Fellingham, Terry Share, Bertie Matthews, Stanley Cotton, David Bailey, John Coe, Derek Lummis, Reg Paske, Gerald Rice, Alan Lee.
Front Row: Teddy Collett, William Arnold, Brian Race, John Mills, Michael Sparkes, Robert Bruce, ? Buckle, Chris Sturgeon.

The Rickinghall team in the 1950s.

From L to R: Back Row: Brian Race, Michael Sparkes, Tony Miller, Stanley Cotton, Christopher Sturgeon, Alec Hubbard.
Front Row: John Coe, Billy Brown, Willy Arnold, Derek Lummis, Will Parkington.

Botesdale Football team 1950s:

From L to R: Back Row: ?Len Garnham, Gerald Amps, Philip Garnham, Unknown, Alfred Bennett, unknown, unknown, John Wilby.
Front Row: Unknown, Denis Simonds, Unknown, Lawrence Flatman, Eric Clark?, John Garnham

The wedding of Alfie Ray and Grace Cotton in December 1949 outside Thelnetham Church. Alfie was the captain of Rickinghall at this time and the team arrived to form a guard of honour having played and won a match.
Left towards church door: Ronnie Francis, Arthur Leggett, Francis Chillistone, Noel Foulger, Paul Stobbe.
Right towards church door: Ronnie Farrow, Peter Cotton, Derek Harvey, Abby Hill, Jack Kemp.

A photograph of Redgrave Rangers from the early 1950s.

Redgrave Rangers in January 1988. The lady in the centre of the photo is Evelyn Taylor who saved the club when it was to close in 1956. Evelyn took over as chairman, secretary and manager. She ran the club until 1981 when her granddaughter Donna took over the roles of treasurer and secretary.

From L to R: Back Row: Mark Taylor, Paul Whorton, Gary Farrow, Charlie Nevitt, Robbie Pretty, Adrian Black, Neville Culley, Donna Taylor.
Middle Row: Mick Capon, Steve Bishop, Roger Nevitt, Evelyn Taylor, Dave Hayward, Andy Stannard, Bruce Maughn.
Front Row: Hughie Taylor, Rick Taylor, Derek Nevitt, Neil Royal.

Redgrave Rangers have won many awards. This photo shows them as Football Shield Winners in 1994 with their shirts sponsored by Button's Poultry farm.

In this later photo their shirts show they are being sponsored by Kerry Foods who bought Button's duck business. The tradition has been continued by Gressingham Foods.

An action shot taken when Redgrave Rangers were playing against Rickinghall.

Cricket being played on Barley Birch sports field in the early 20th century.

Some of the cricket team in the 1930s.
From L to R: Back Row: Unknown, unknown, unknown
Middle Row: Stephen Warren, unknown, Leonard Wilson (Rector), George Rowland Holt Wilson (Squire).
Front Row: Noel Warren, unknown, unknown, Alec Davey wicket keeper, unknown.

Bowls at The Bell Hotel around 1954 -1955.

From L to R: Back Row: Edwin Kerry, Dennis Collins, ? Perry, Unknown, Mr Scott, Noel Warren.
Middle Row: Unknown, Unknown, Unknown, Mr Scott, Alec Davey, Mr Shaw, Revd Cotton, Cyril Perry, Unknown, Unknown.
Front Row: Unknown, Stanley Perry, unknown, Mr Collins.

Rickinghall bowls team, the 1970 League Cup winners. At this time the bowling green was behind Jessamine House.

From L to R: Back Row: Fred Miller, Harry Bath, Sam Ramsey, Keith Miller, Noel Warren, Ellen and Bert Matthews.
Front Row: Ashley Flatman, John Mills, Fred Palistange, Jack and Olwynne Miller, Teddy Collett.

The Cock pub darts team in the early 1950s.
From L to R: Back Row: Geoff Lister, Alf Ramsey, ? Shore, Frederick Moore, unknown.
Front Row: George Huggins, Percy Norman, Charlie Carver (landlord) Fred Churchyard, Bob Huggins.

Lord Playfair, who was renting Redgrave Hall, with other participants at a shooting party in the early 20th century.

Chapter 12
Redgrave Hall and Park

Sir Nicholas Bacon bought the Manor of Redgrave from King Henry VIII in 1542 after the dissolution of the monasteries. The building commissioned by Abbot Samson in 1211 was demolished and replaced with a Tudor style house completed in 1554 at a cost of £1253.2.5¾. Two further wings were added to this house in about 1676. Robert Bacon sold the Manor to Sir John Holt in 1702.

Frontispiece of Redgrave Estate Book drawn up for the then owner Admiral Wilson in 1803.

Rowland Holt III 1723 – 1786. His father died suddenly when Rowland was only 16. He was succeeded by his brother Thomas who died in 1799.

Lucinda Holt, elder sister of Rowland and Thomas, married Thomas Wilson. Their son Admiral George Wilson inherited the estate as Thomas Holt had no heir.

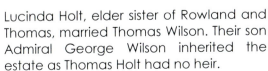

Map of Redgrave Park from Redgrave Estate Book of 1803.

This early photograph, taken mid-19th century, shows a man in a stove pipe hat looking across the lake to Redgrave Hall.

Henry Horsfall leased Redgrave Hall from 1895 -1898. His wife Violet bred great danes and was a judge at Crufts dog shows. These photographs appeared in Country Life Illustrated in 1897 when an article was written about Violet. (See photograph on page 195).

Redgrave Hall.

Orangery.

Ancient trees in Redgrave Park.

Redgrave Hall in the early 20th century with horses grazing nearby.

The Welsh Horse Yeomanry in Redgrave Park about 1915. (See page 11).

Rowland Holt III commissioned Lancelot 'Capability' Brown in 1767 to redesign the Tudor house built for Sir Nicholas Bacon and change it to a classical style. He also widened and dammed the stream running through the park to form a serpentine lake. This postcard is postmarked 1909.

Redgrave Hall and lake.

This photograph clearly shows the porch which had been added to the classical portico of the house.

In the early 1930s Redgrave Hall and Park were let for use as a country club.

Below is a set of photographs taken in the 1930s when John Holt Wilson intended to let Redgrave Hall.

Meat larder in the yard.

These photographs, taken at the same time and part of the previous set, show the interior of the drawing room.

The drawing room fireplace.

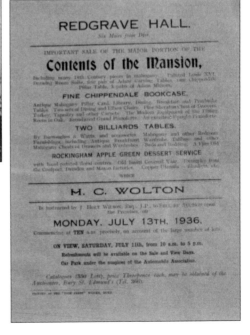

Auction catalogue dated 1936 when John Holt Wilson sold the furniture.

Redgrave Hall and Park was requisitioned when WWII began in 1939. At first the hall itself was occupied by various military units. When Redgrave Park was occupied by temporary American hospitals the hall itself was not used and the windows were shuttered, as can be seen in this photograph.

Redgrave Hall in the snow.

The medical staff of the 231st Station Hospital felt cold in their huts even before the snow arrived.

Nurse and patient enjoying the snow.

Rehabilitation Ward.

Ambulance outside the neurosurgical ward. The most severely injured patients were brought from other hospitals by ambulance or hospital trains which arrived at local railway stations.

The 231st Station Hospital arrived in October 1943 and was moved to Wymondham in February 1944. The 65th General Hospital moved to Redgrave Park in February and March 1944. In the twenty months that the 65th were in Redgrave Park they handled 17,250 bed patients and 30,000 outpatients.

Neurosurgical Ward.

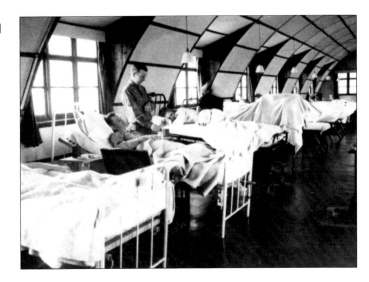

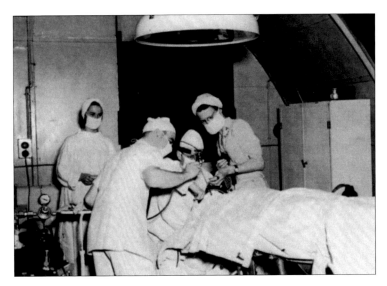

Operating Theatre.

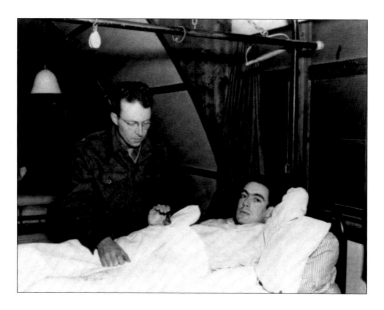

Patient showing Maj. Jacobs a piece of metal removed in an operation.

Walkway between wards.

Three different 65th General Hospital signs at the entrance gates and lodge.

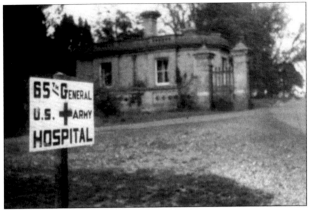

Signpost to the hospital in front of Knoll Cottage, Redgrave. This photograph may have been taken between VE day, 8th May 1945, the end of the war in Europe, and before the American hospital staff left after VJ day in August 1945, the end of the war in Japan, as signposts would have been removed during the war.

Nurses wearing their gas masks.

Leaving the wash-room was cold in winter for the nurses walking back to their huts and they often only had cold water to wash with.

Climbing on an ancient oak in Redgrave Park. The tree may date back to the medieval period when the area was the Abbot's deer park.

Cycles were necessary to get around the camp and for leisure time on days off.

Several weddings between hospital staff took place in the chapel at the hospital with some of the brides wearing their uniforms to get married. One couple were married in St Mary's Church, Redgrave and the guests, bridesmaid and page boy had to walk through Redgrave Park and a field to get there.

View of prisoner of war camp which was situated between the lake and the main road in Botesdale. This photograph was taken from the hospital side of the lake.

Prisoners of war working in the gardens of their camp.

Many of the prisoners walked to the local farms where they worked. They made wooden toys and gave them to the children they met on the way. A few prisoners lived in the homes of the farmers they worked for and there were strict regulations which the farmers had to abide by. The prisoners were allowed to walk unescorted and visit local homes within a radius of five miles but had to guard against 'relationships of an amorous nature developing between the prisoners and local women.'

Prefabricated huts in which the prisoners lived. These photographs were taken from the top of the water tower which is the only reminder of the POW camp still standing.

Redgrave Hall was sold off at an auction for building materials in 1946. When Capability Brown designed the Palladian hall he demolished two wings which had been added to the house in the 17th century but he retained the original hall as a kitchen at the rear

of the classical hall. He used white brick as a skin to cover the red brick of the remaining wings of the old hall.

This picture shows clearly how the old hall had been adapted. John Holt Wilson intended to restore the old part of the hall as a house to live in, but Redgrave Hall and Park were sold in 1970 and the remaining part demolished.

The gamekeeper's house could be seen from the hall. It was designed by Capability Brown with the end of the house facing Redgrave Hall built to look like a classical folly, although the rest of the building was an ordinary house. It was called The Water House and was opposite the boat house at the far end of the lake. A building called the Dog Kennel was situated next to the gamekeeper's house.

The doorway of the kitchen was the original entrance into the Tudor hall. Above the door is the stone tablet originally placed there by Sir Nicholas Bacon, before he was knighted in 1558.

An advert for a fireplace originally sold at the auction in 1946 appeared in Collectors' Guide in April 1947.

Stoneware originally in Redgrave Park photographed at Green Farm, Redgrave, Peter Holt-Wilson's last home.

The Water Carrier (left). Winter, the only one left of a set of four seasons (right).

Plant holder (left). One of the balls decorating the front garden wall before Redgrave Park was landscaped and Redgrave Hall re-designed by Capability Brown (right).

This little building was designed by Capability Brown. It is marked as a pigeon house on a plan of 1801, but in 1851 it was lived in by the estate carpenter and called Dove House. When this photo was taken in the 1950s it was known as The Duffy House. 'The Temple' is a name used by Brown for this design used on other estates. It has also been called 'The Round House'.

Aerial view of Redgrave Park in 2007.